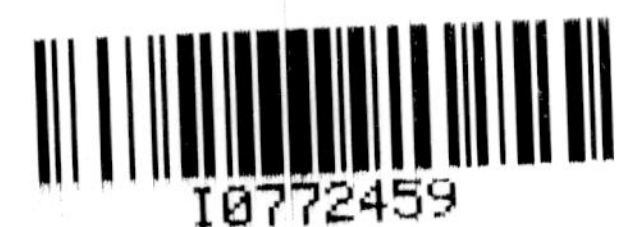

Cute tiny cats coloring book

F. FRANKLIN

Testing page

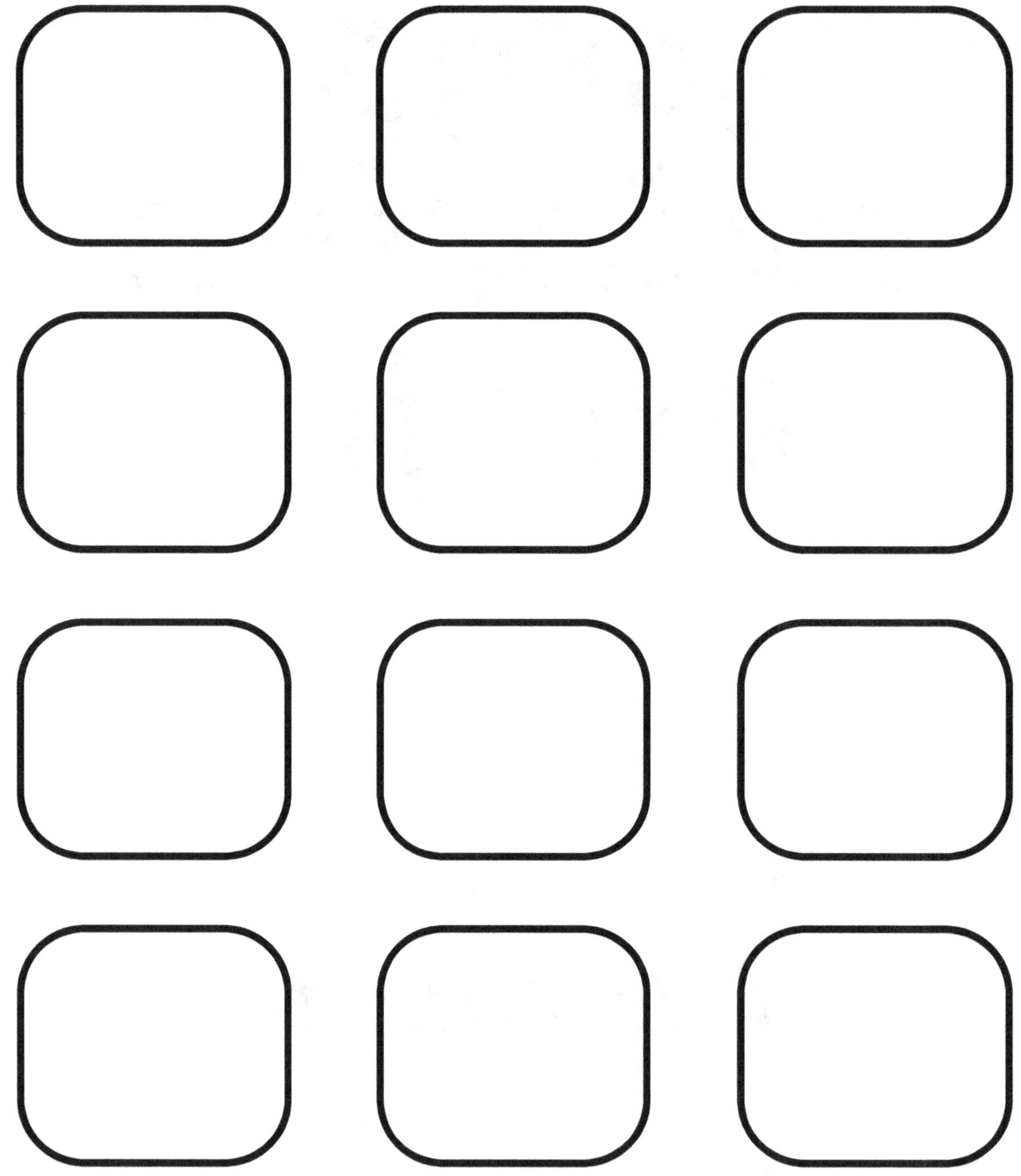

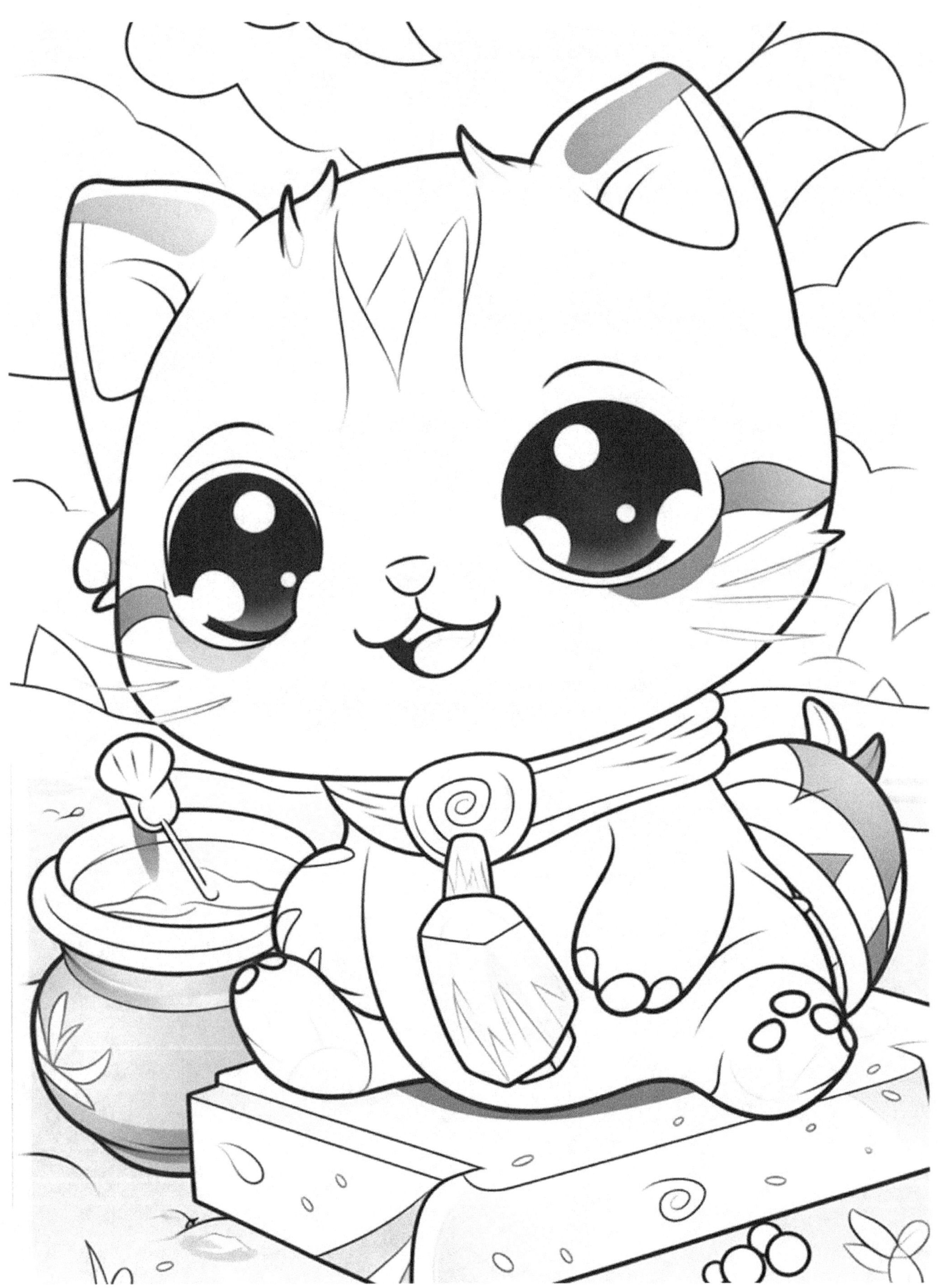

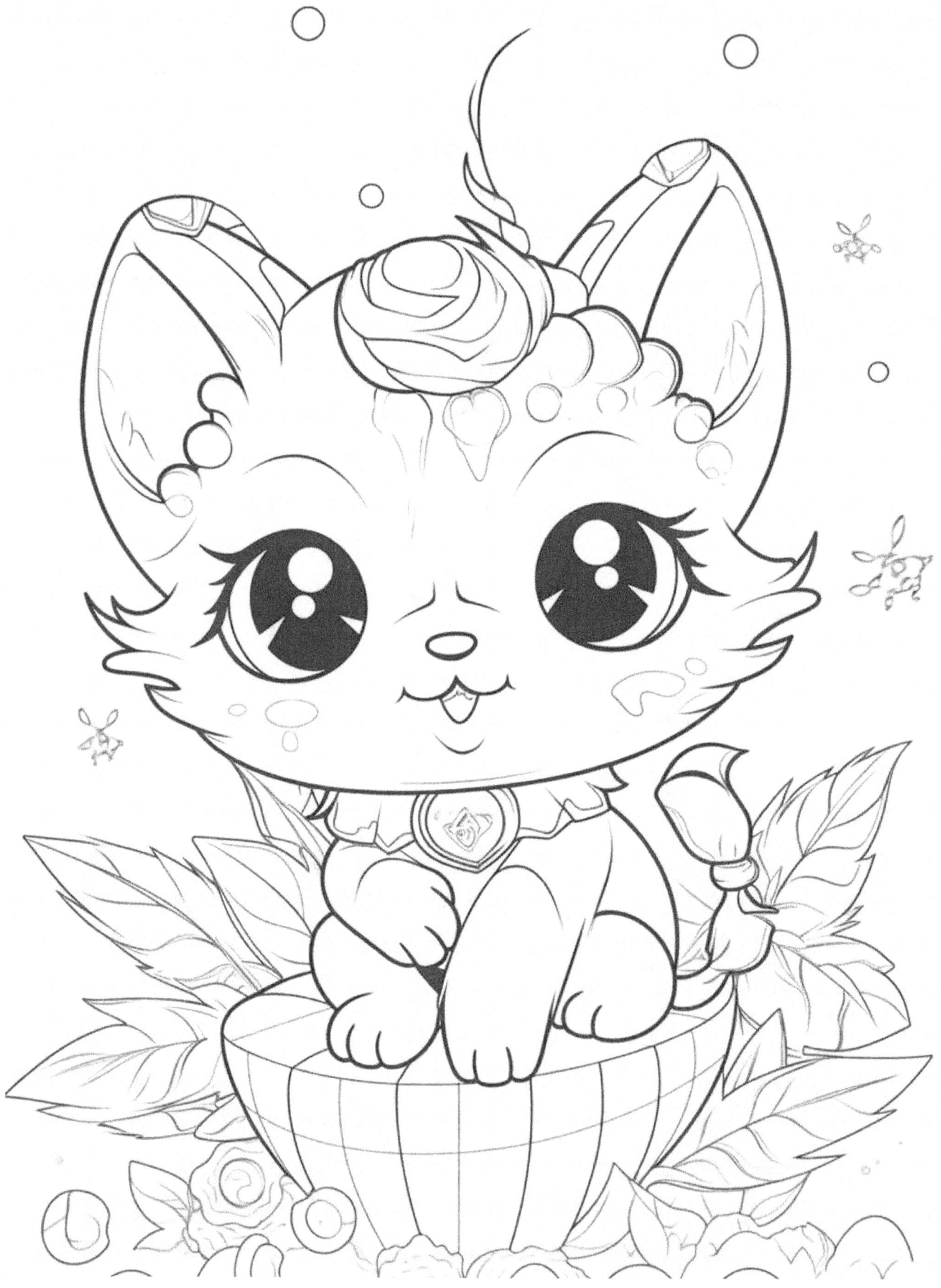

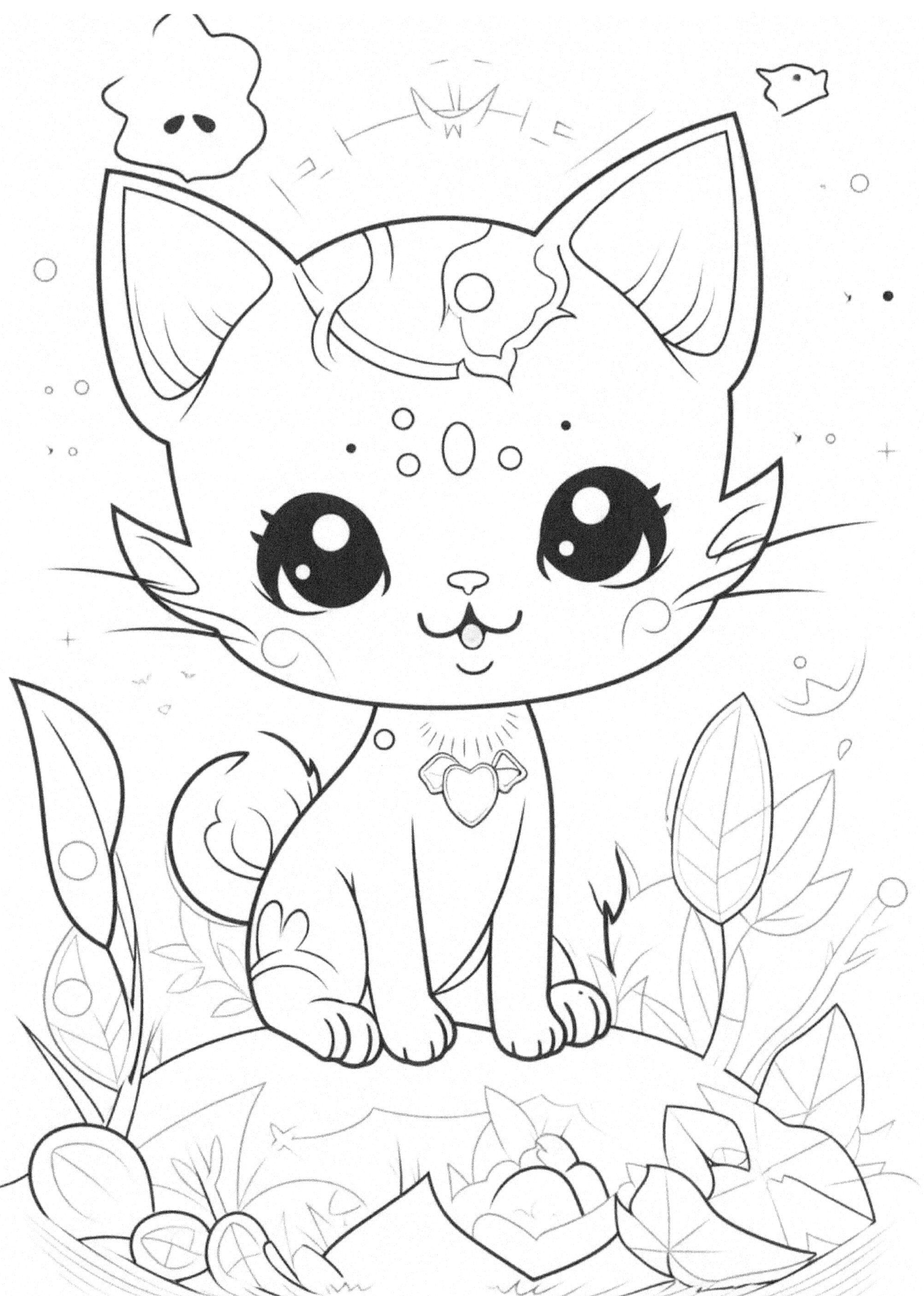

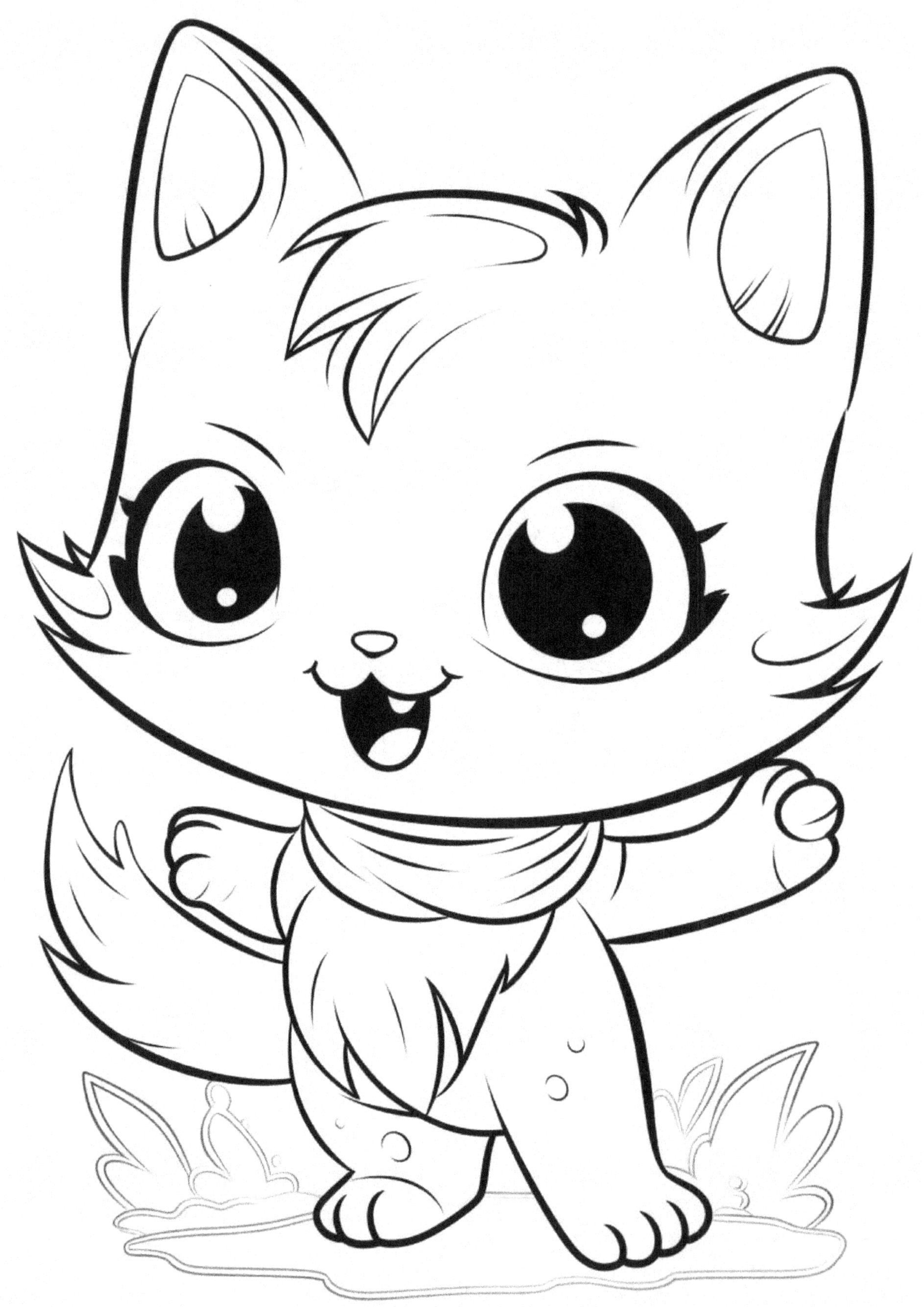

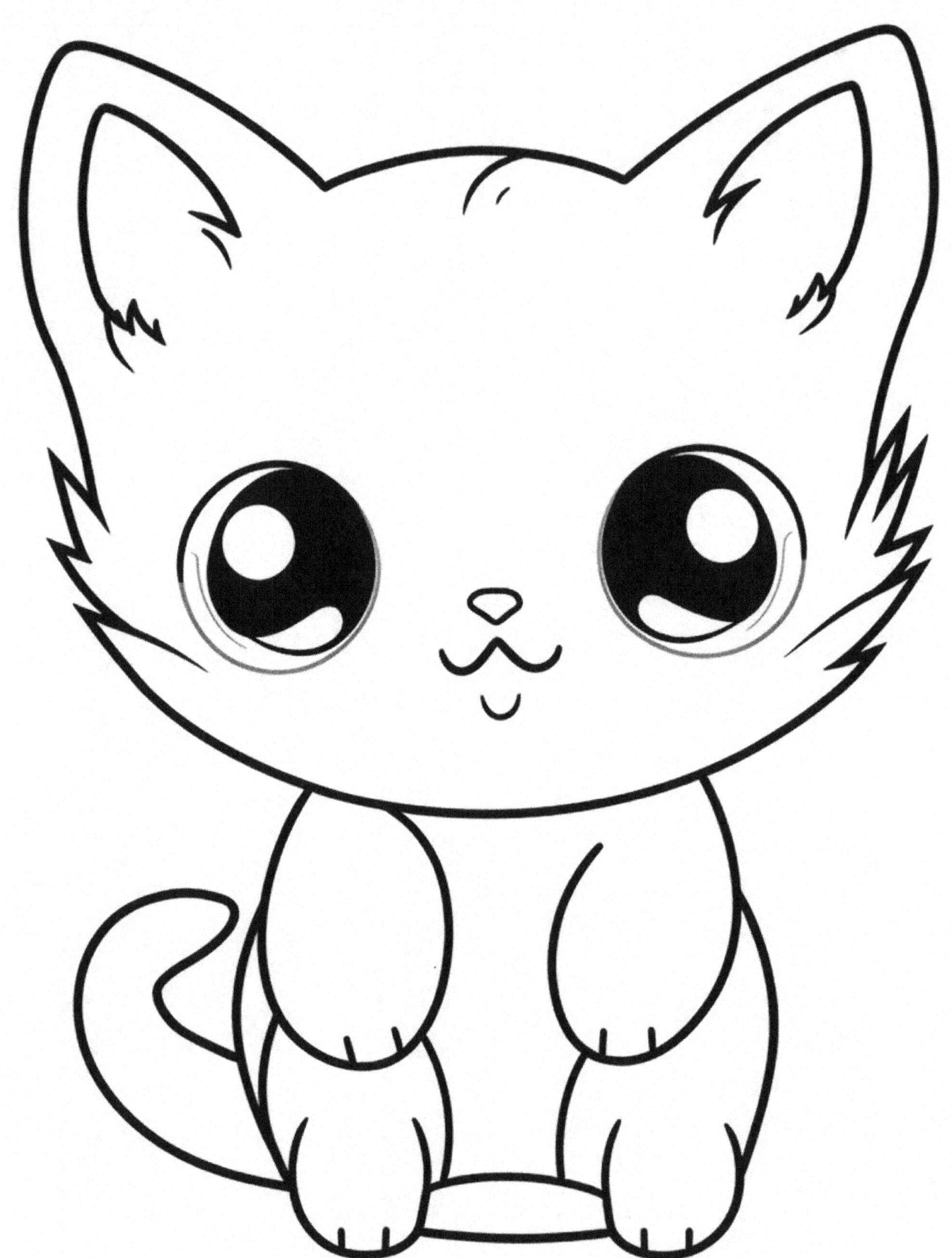

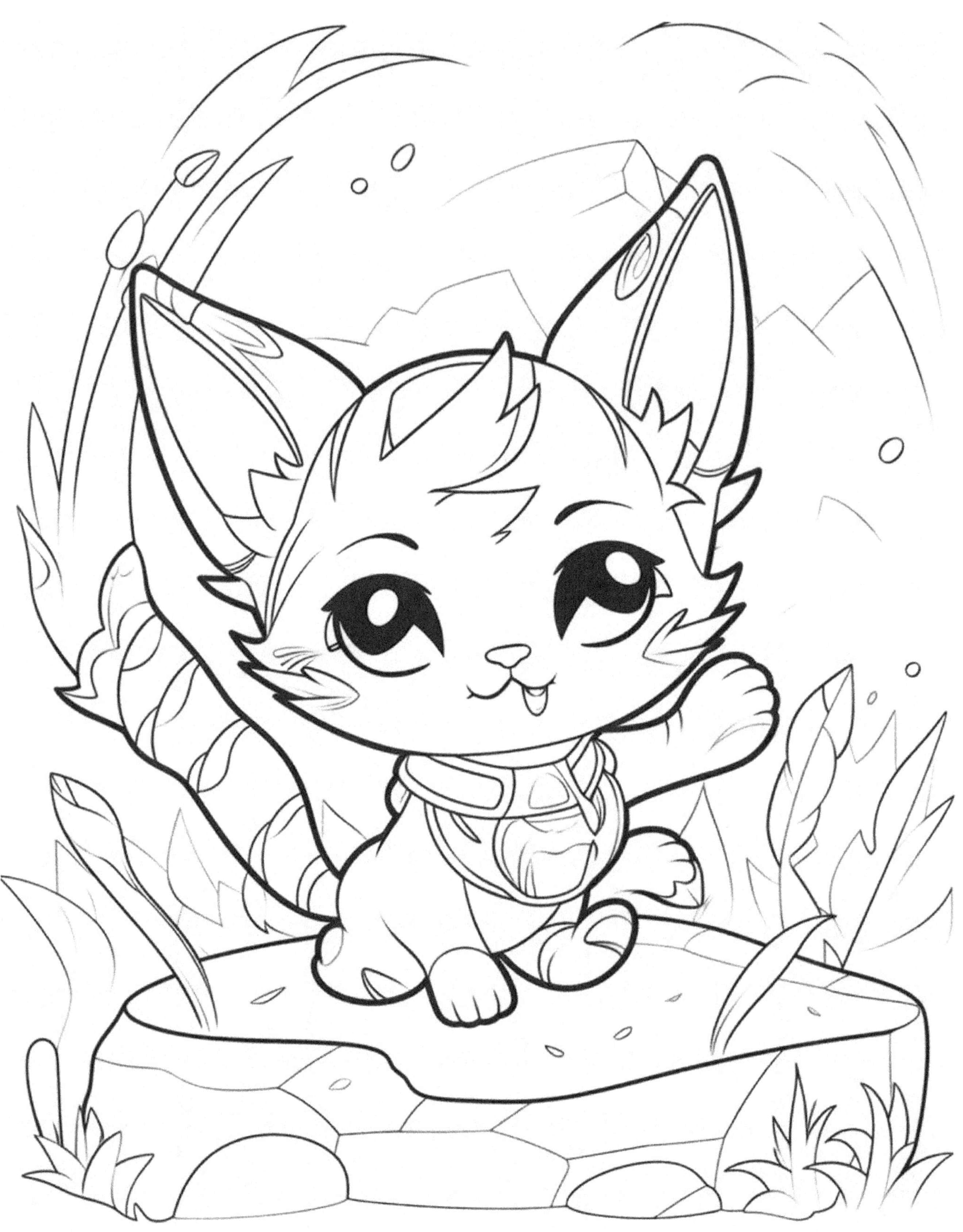

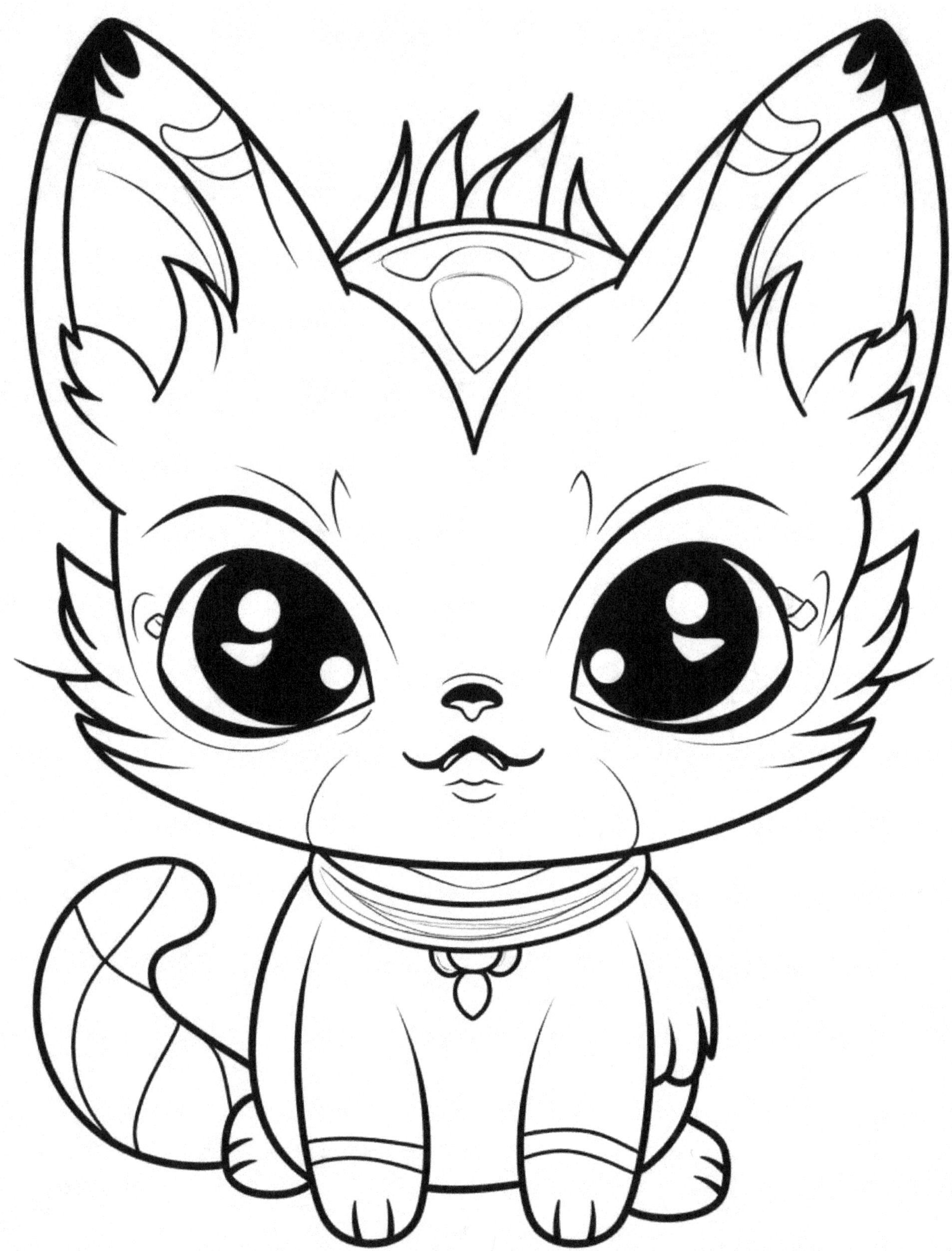

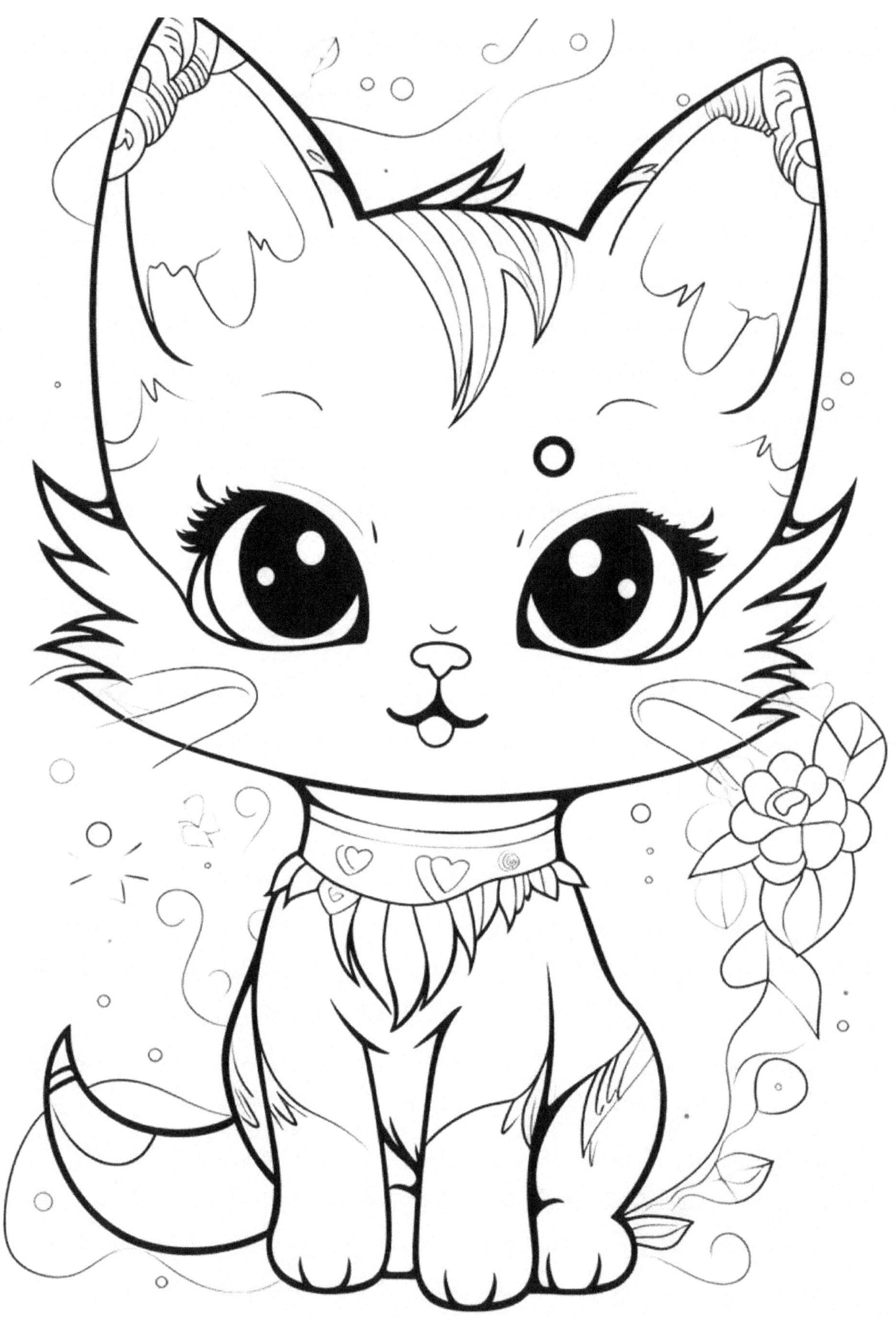

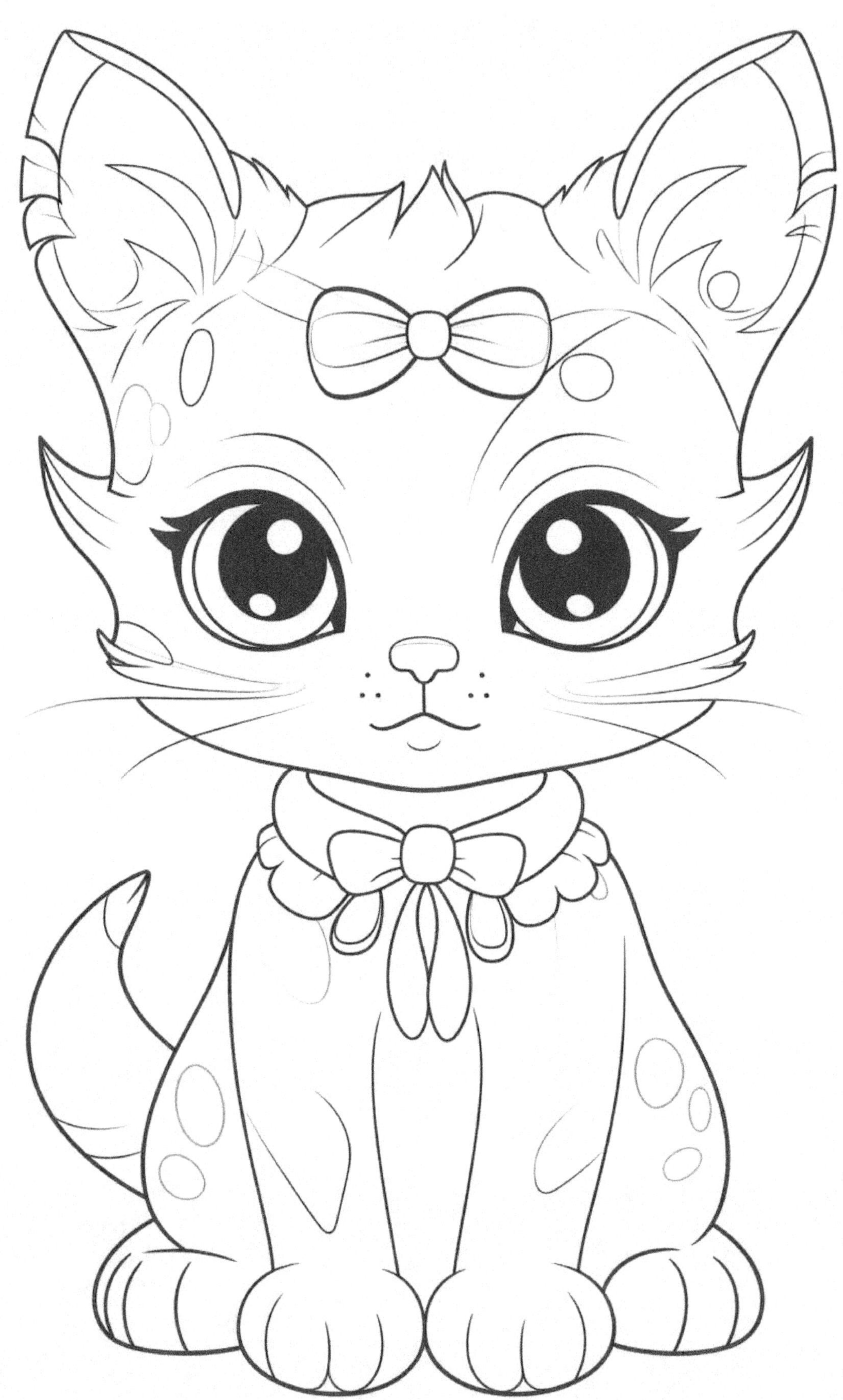

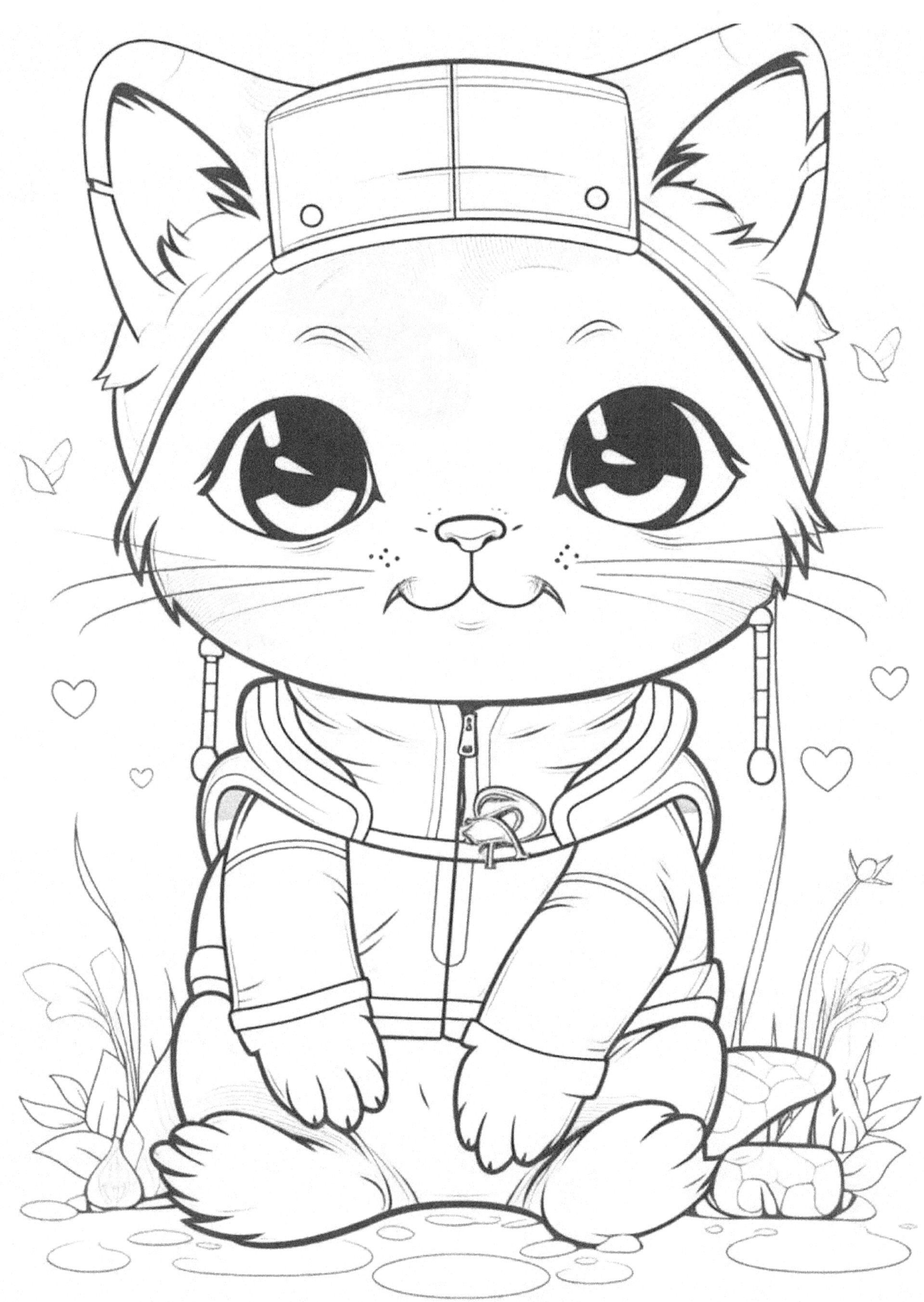

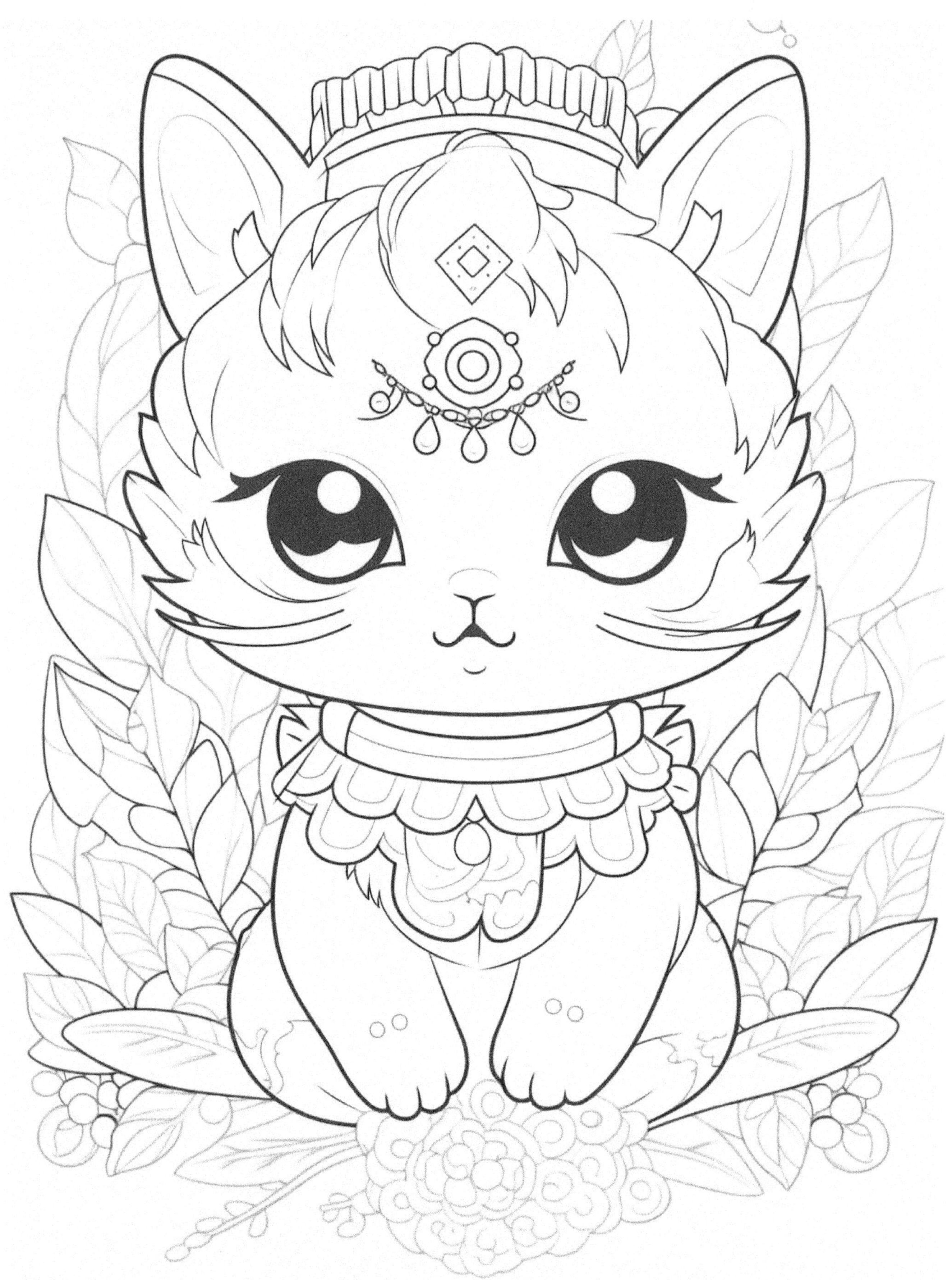

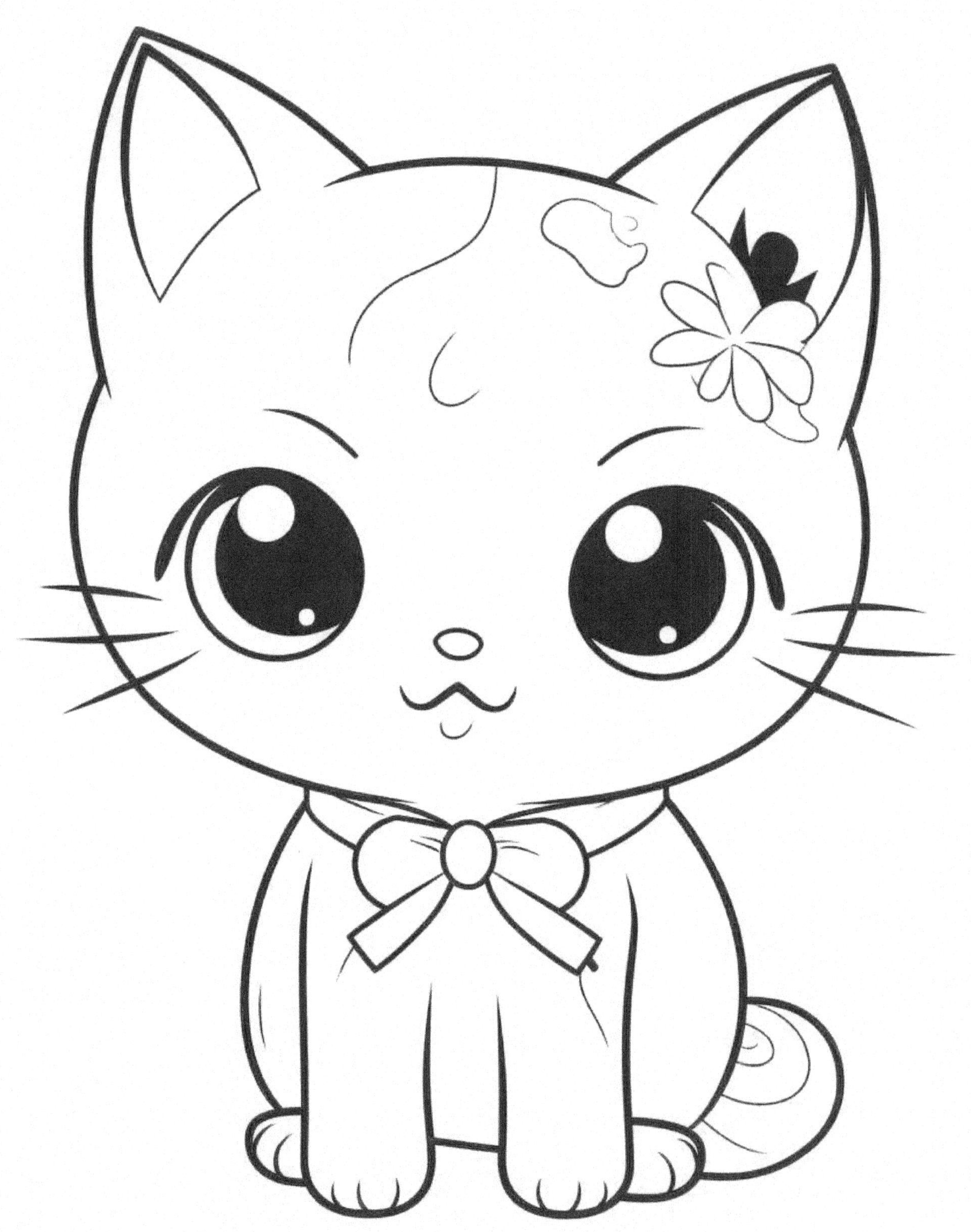

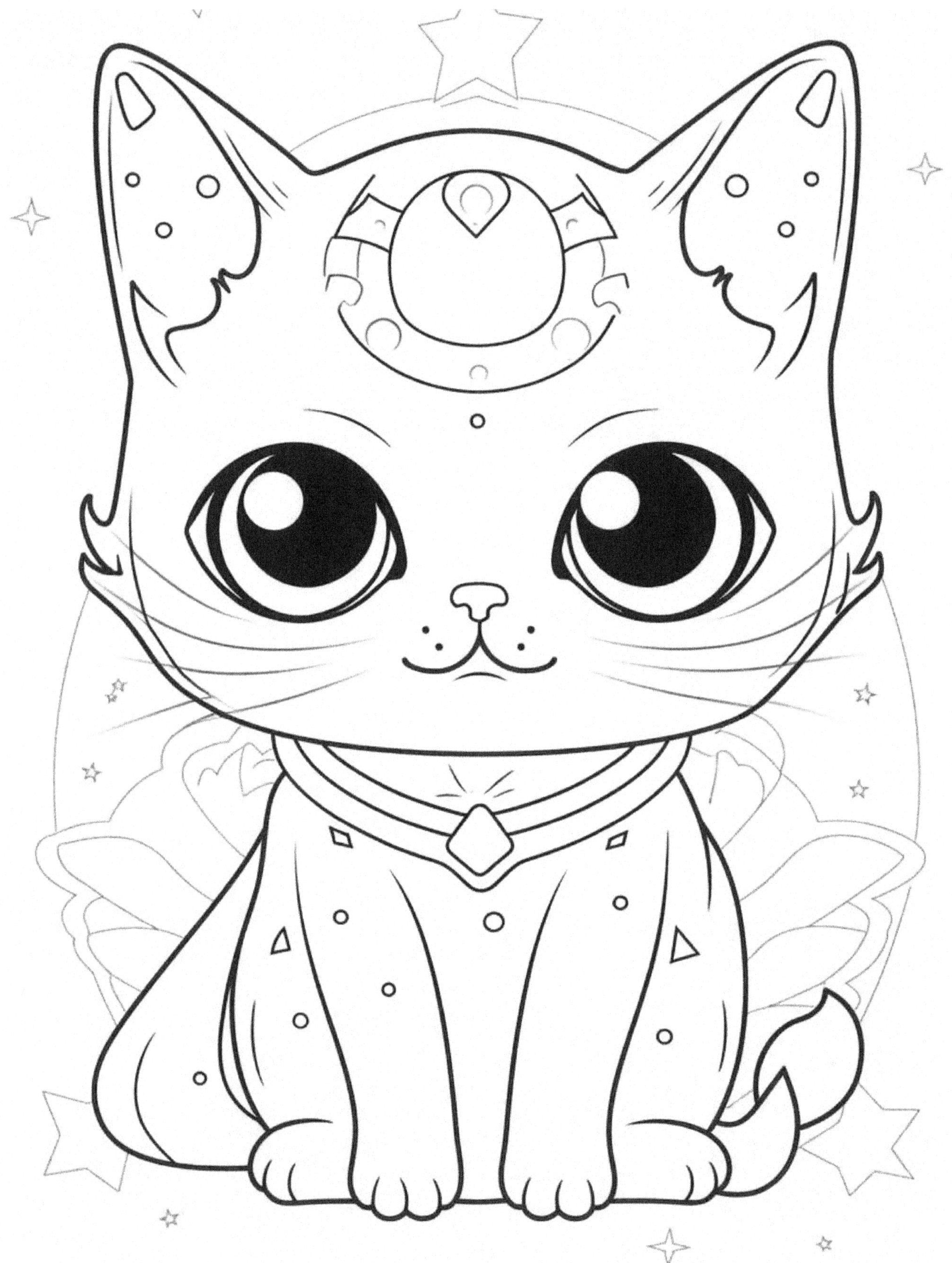

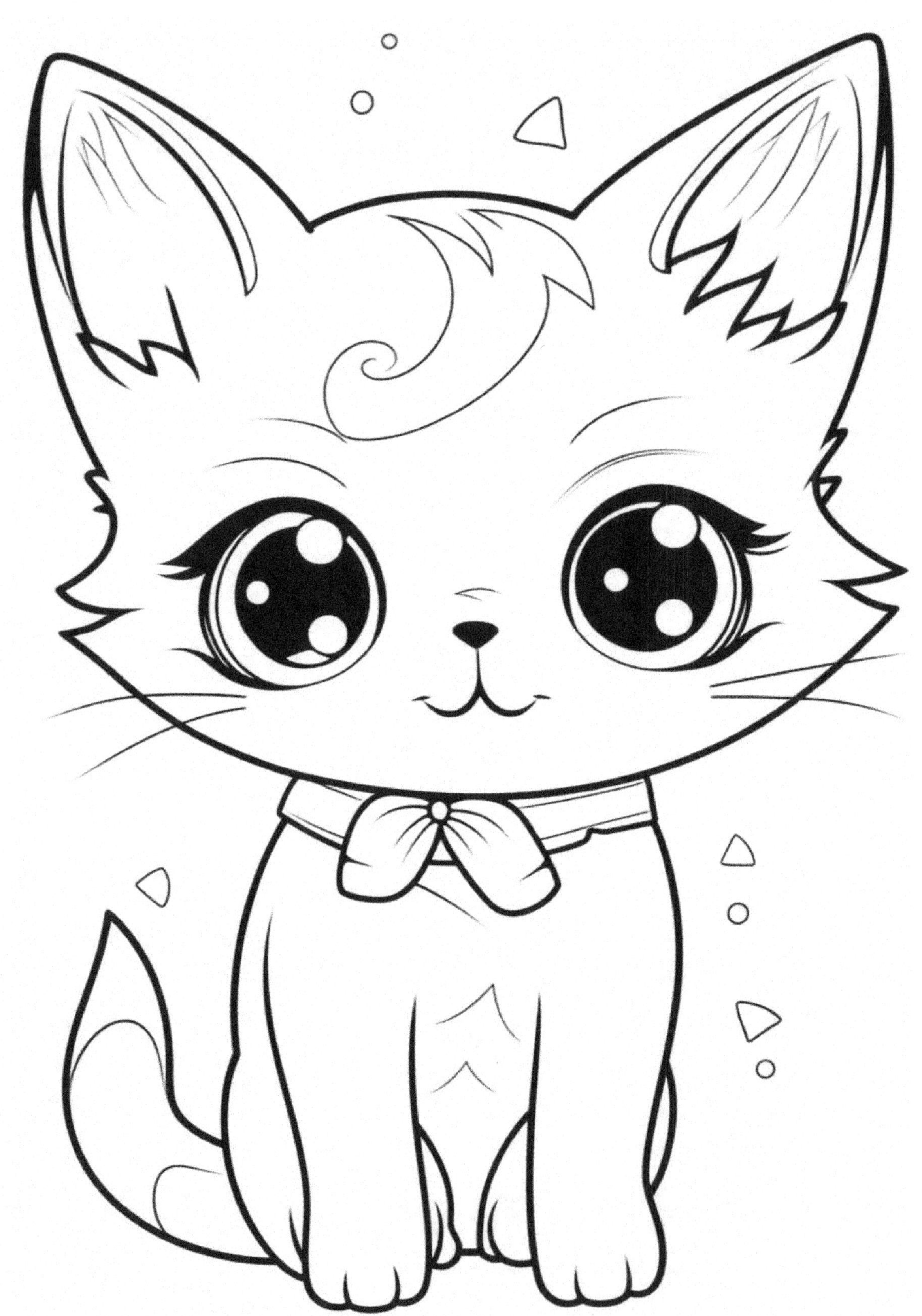

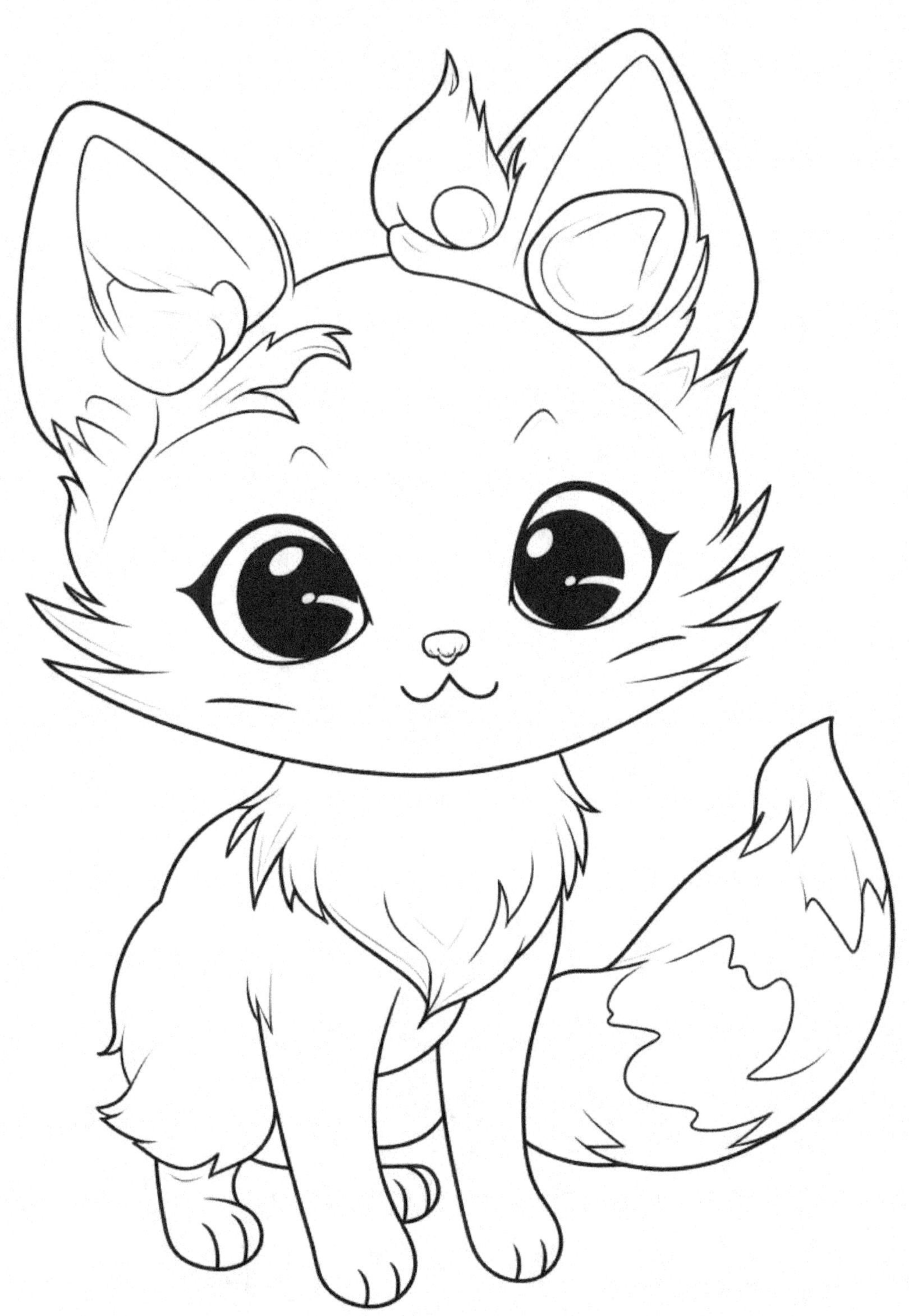

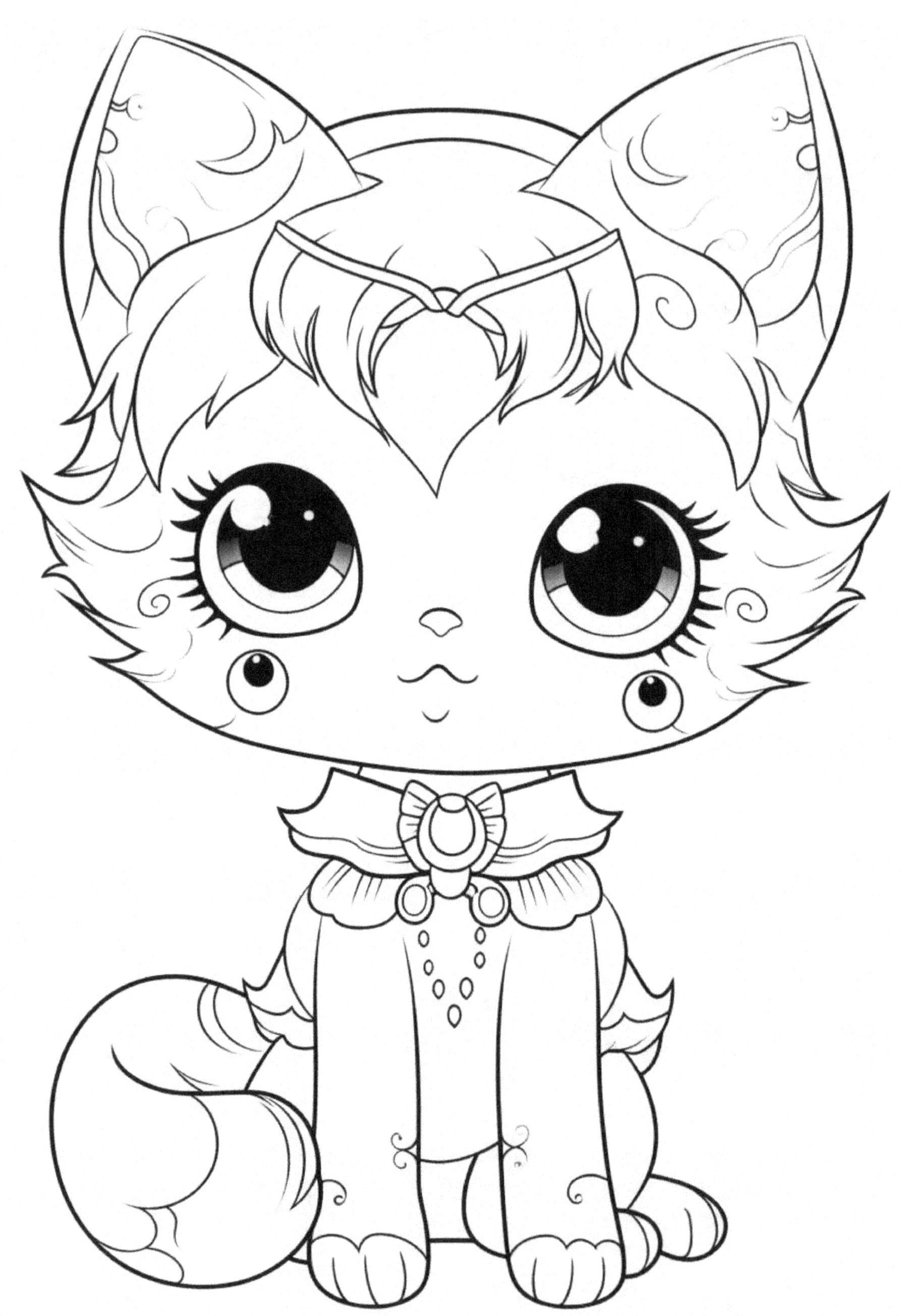

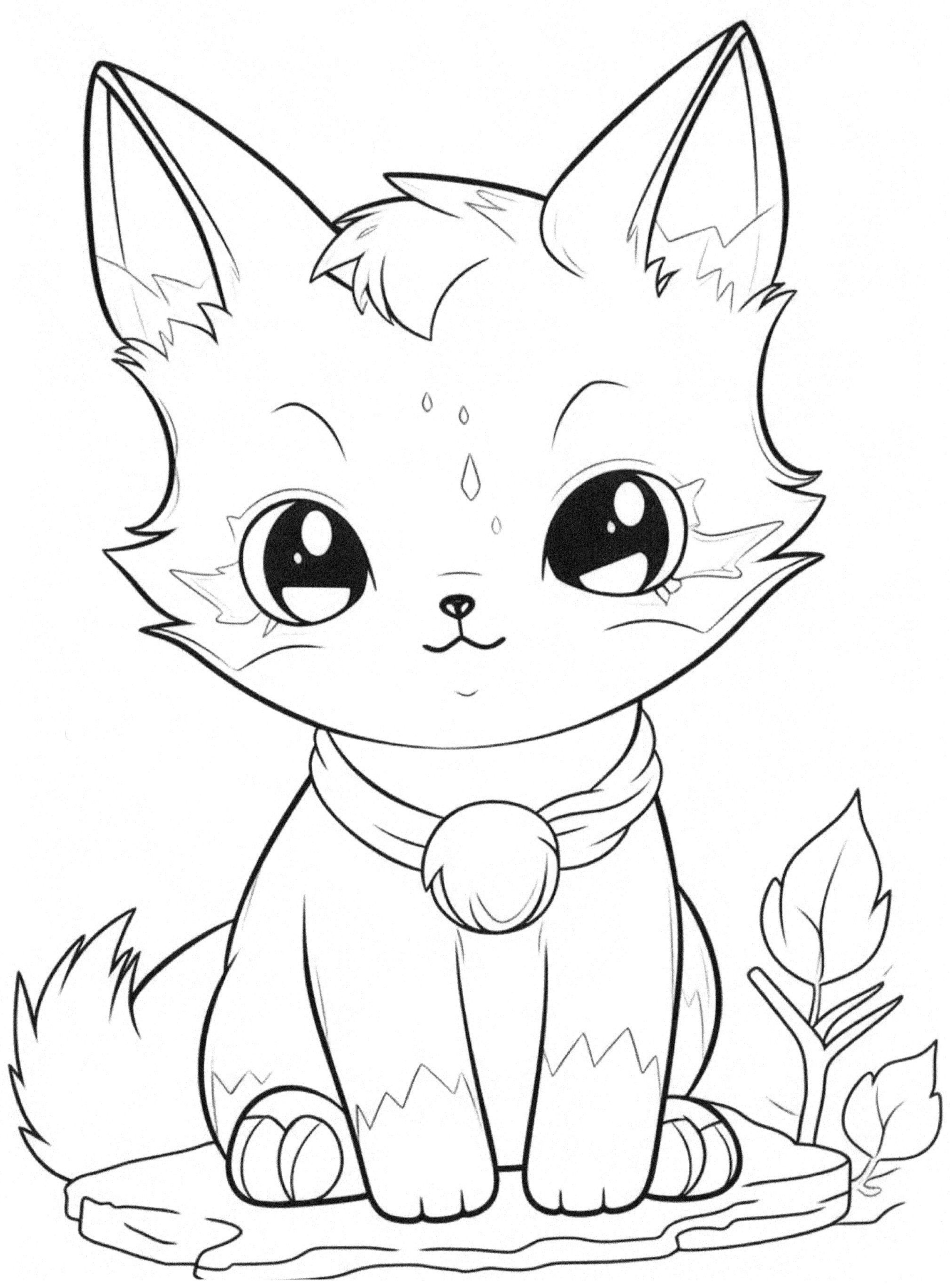

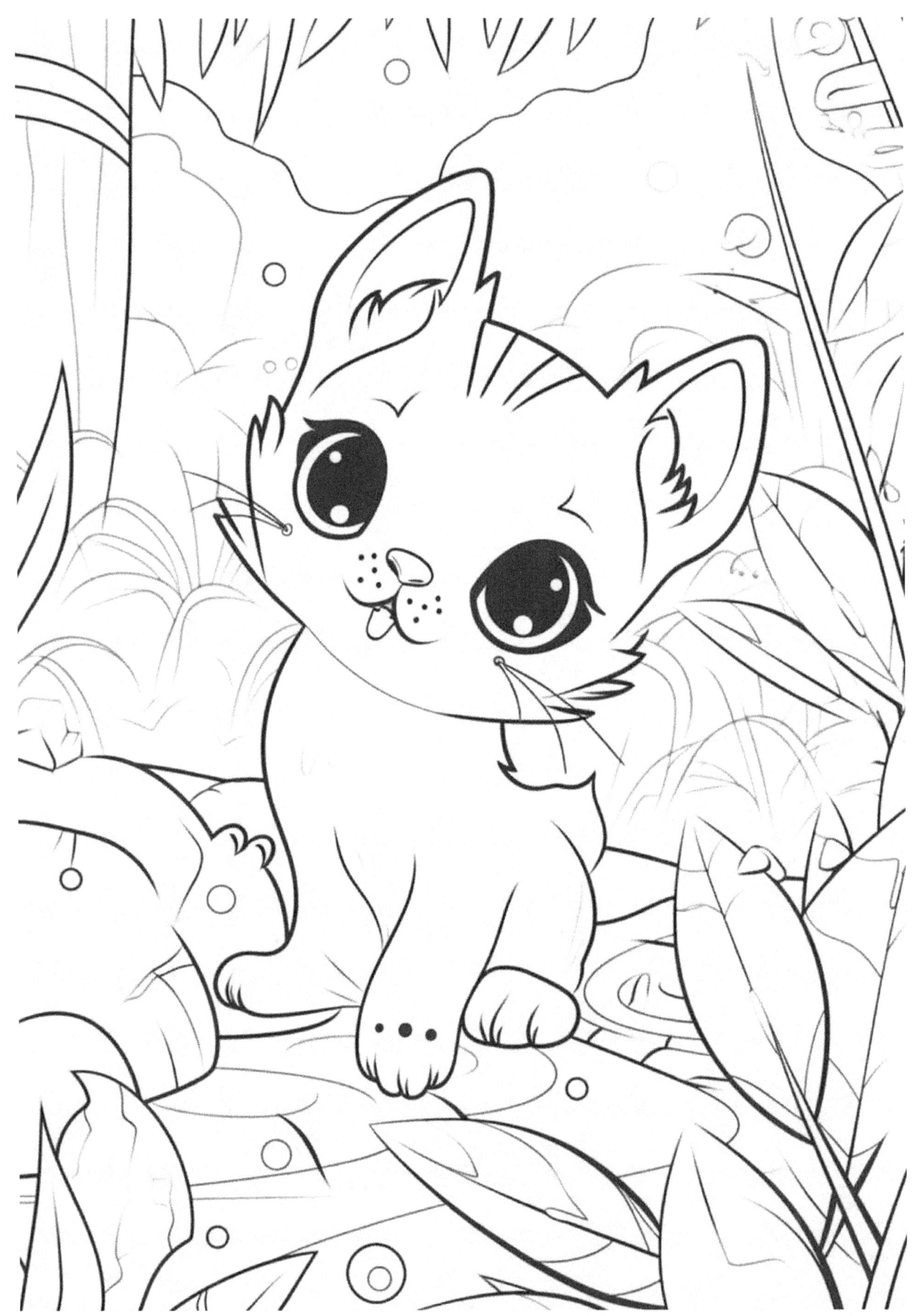

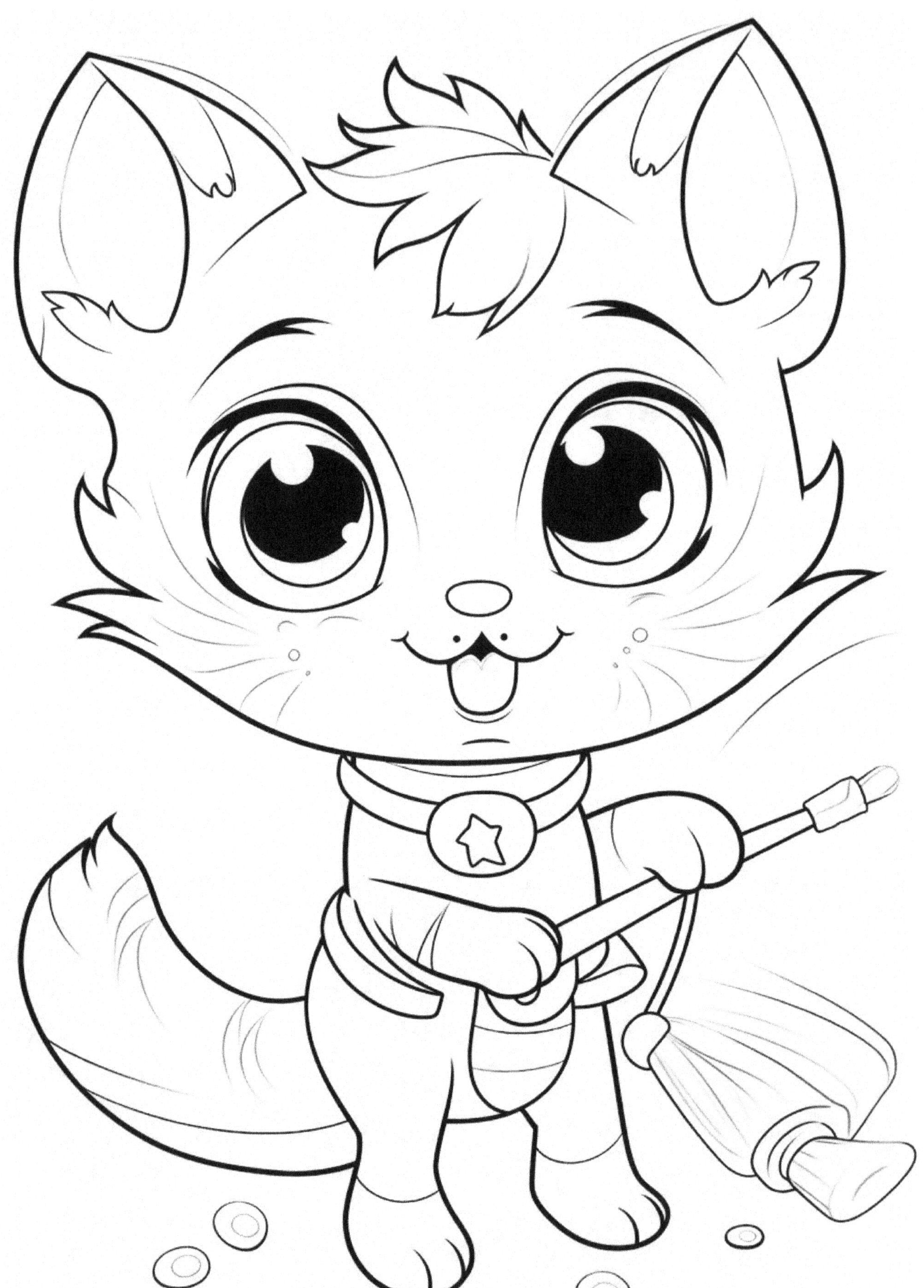

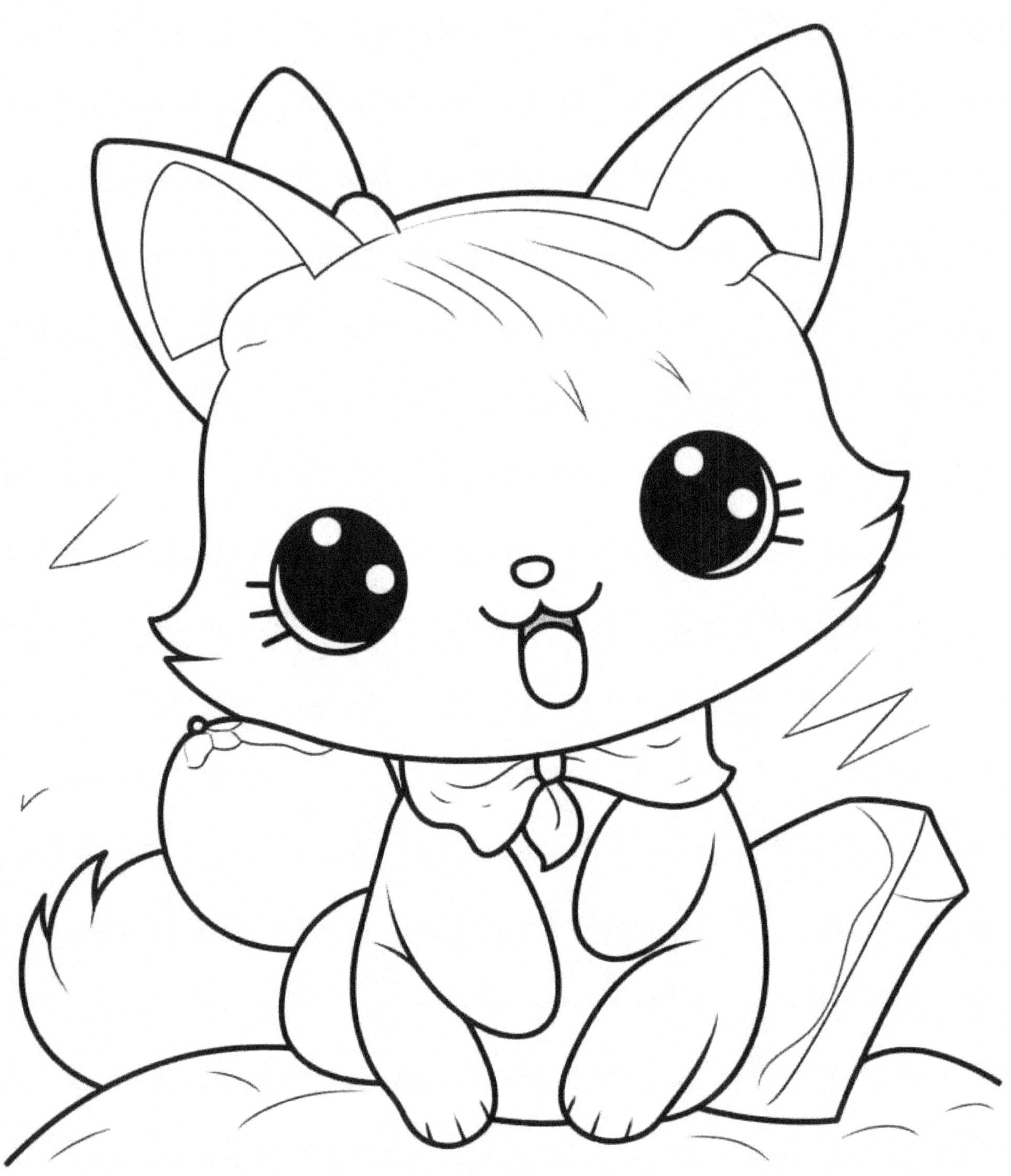

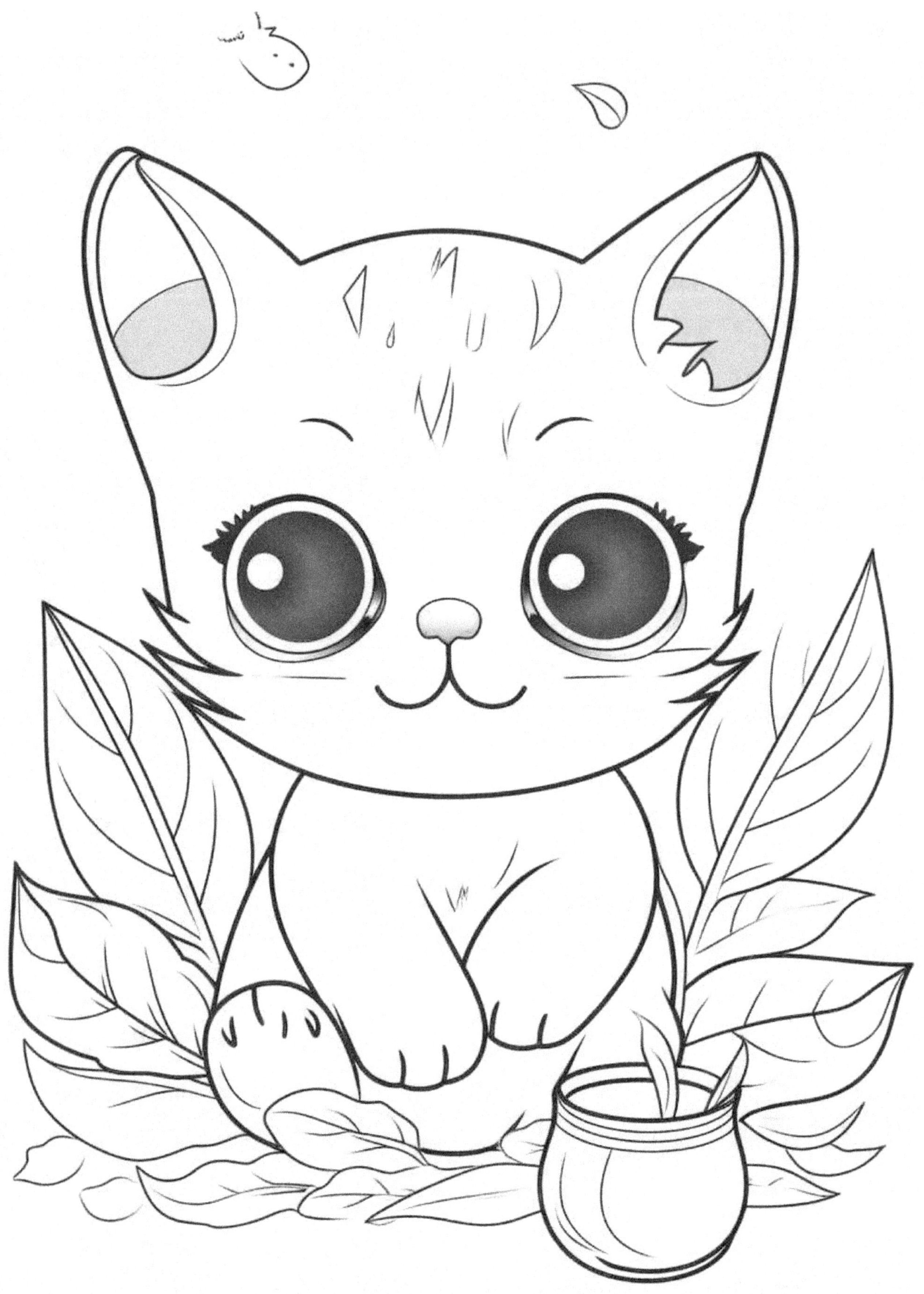

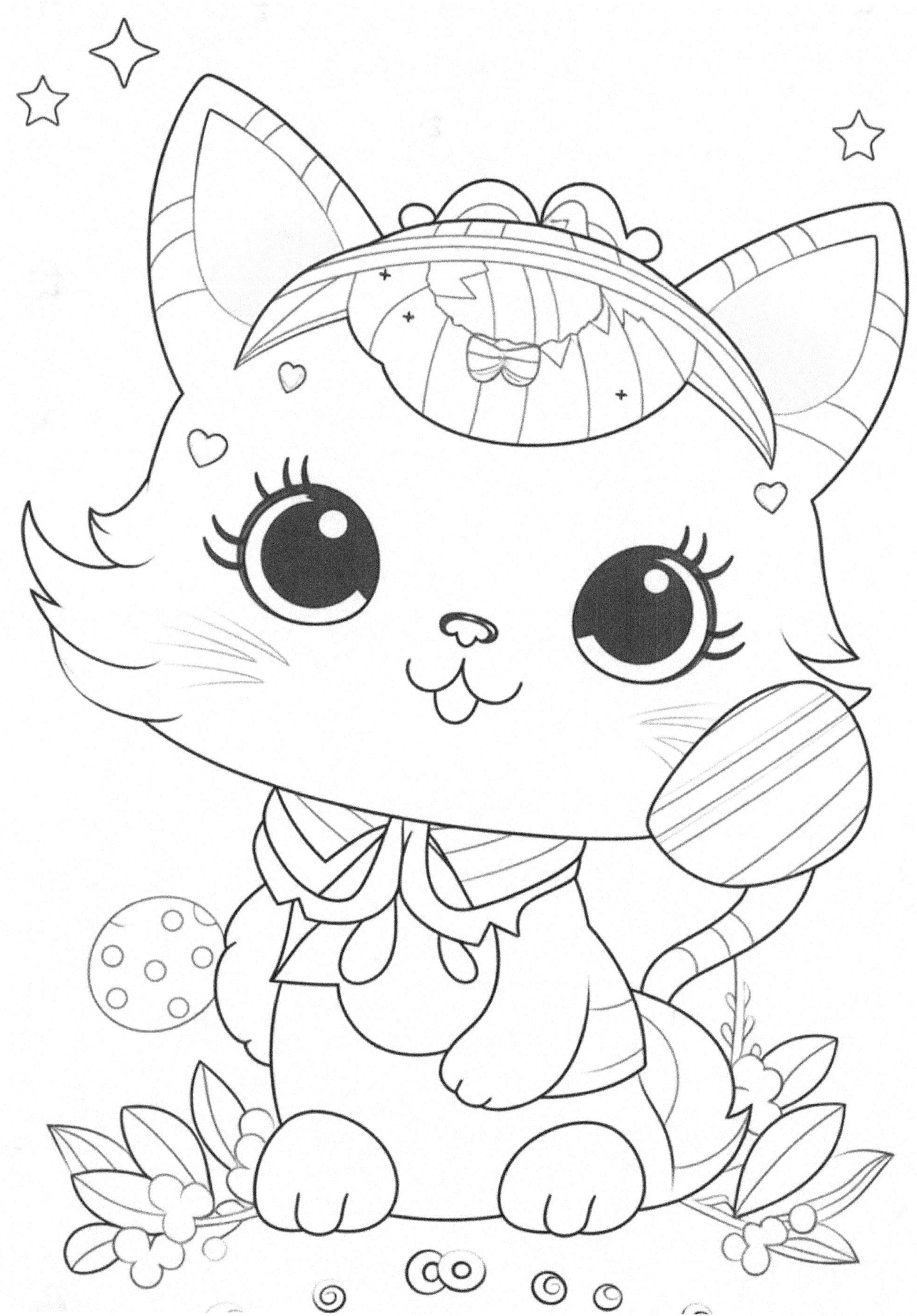

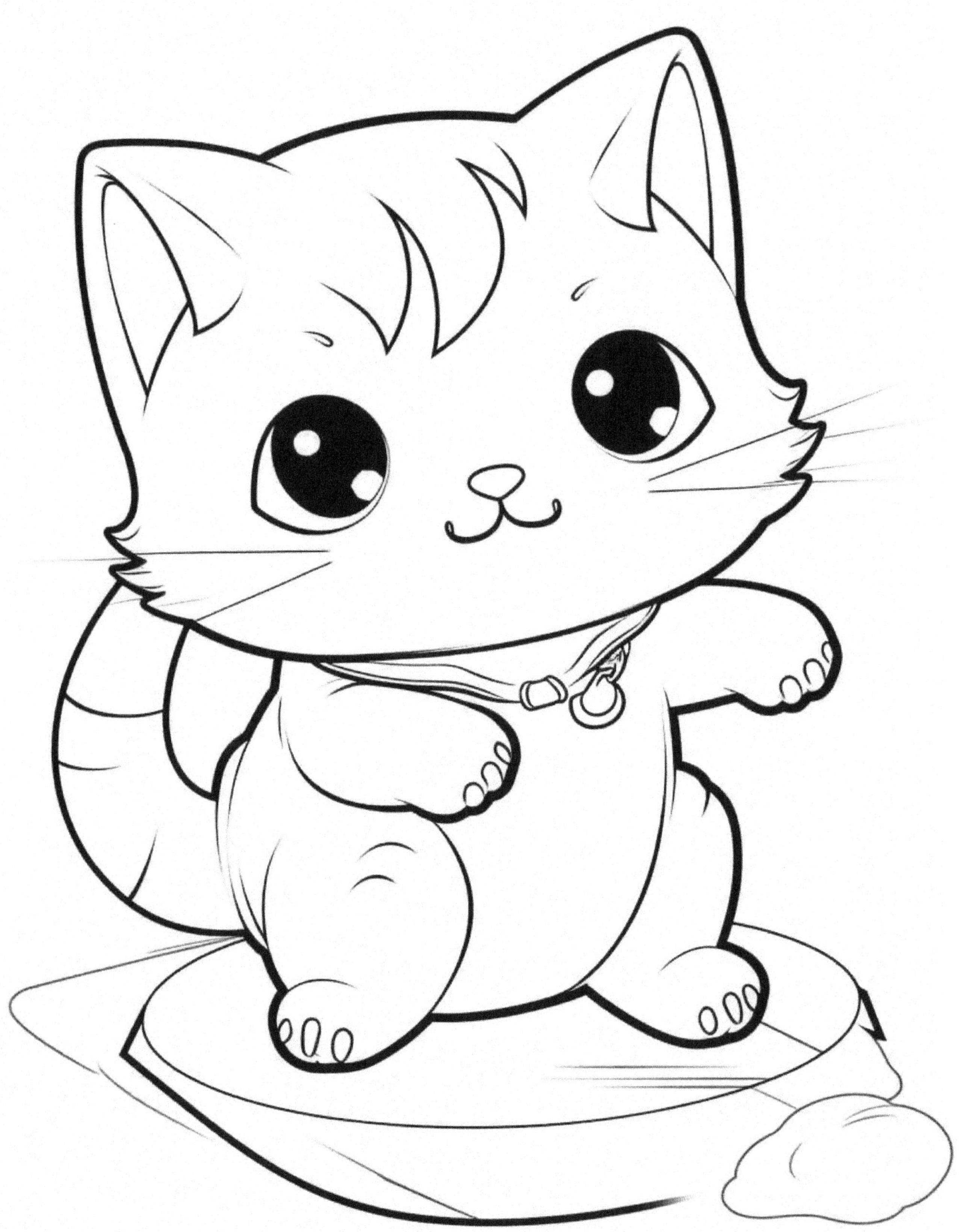

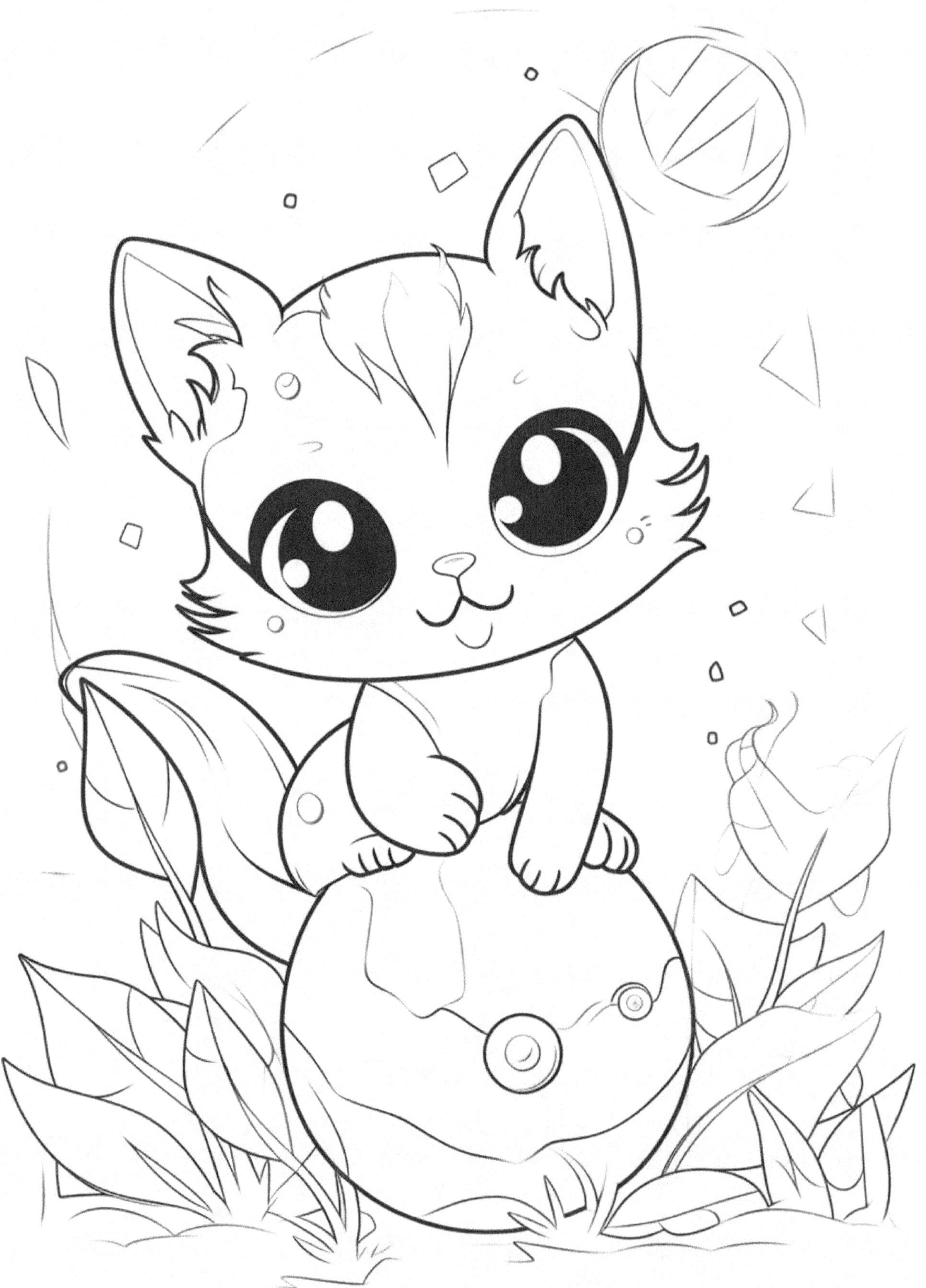

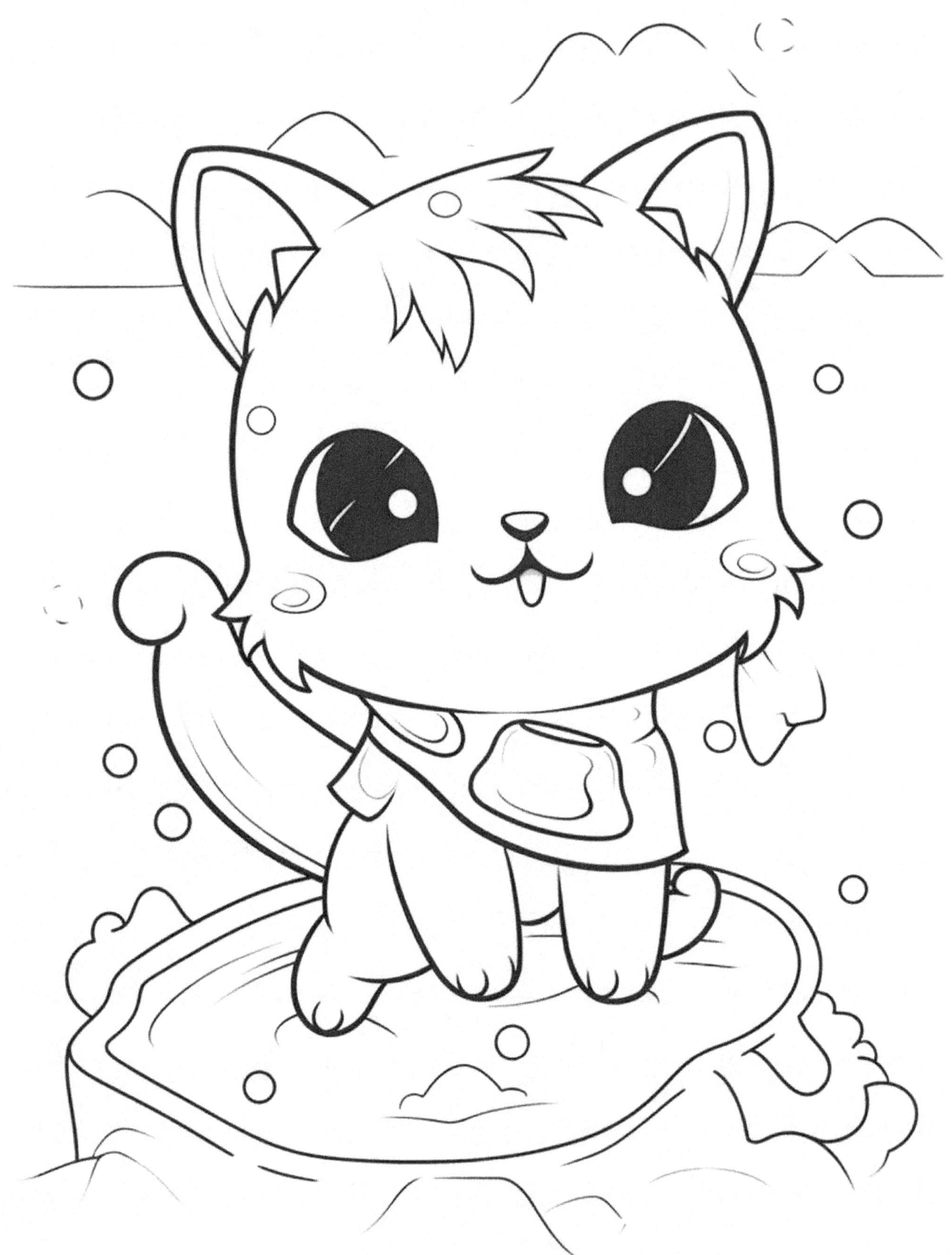

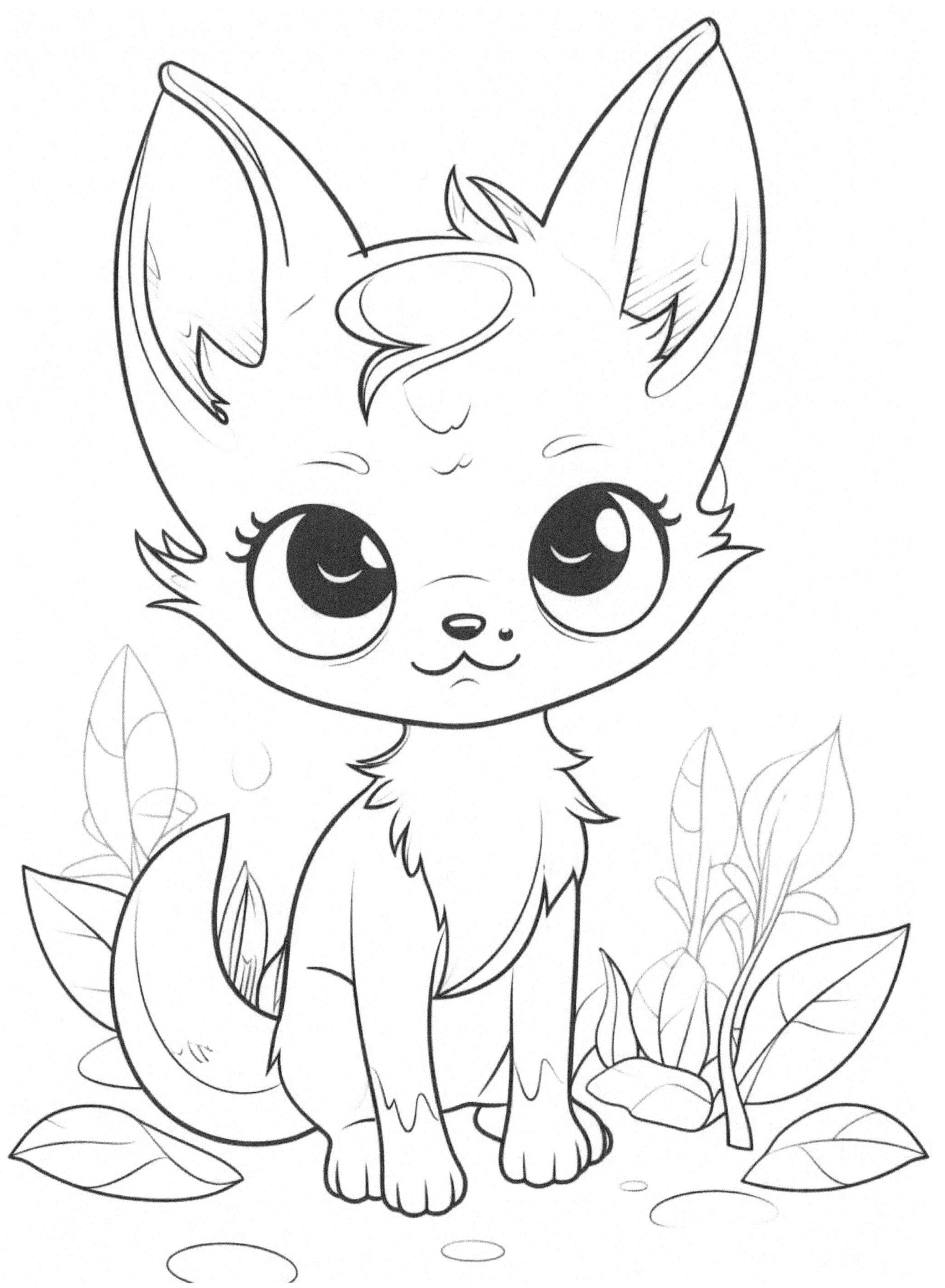

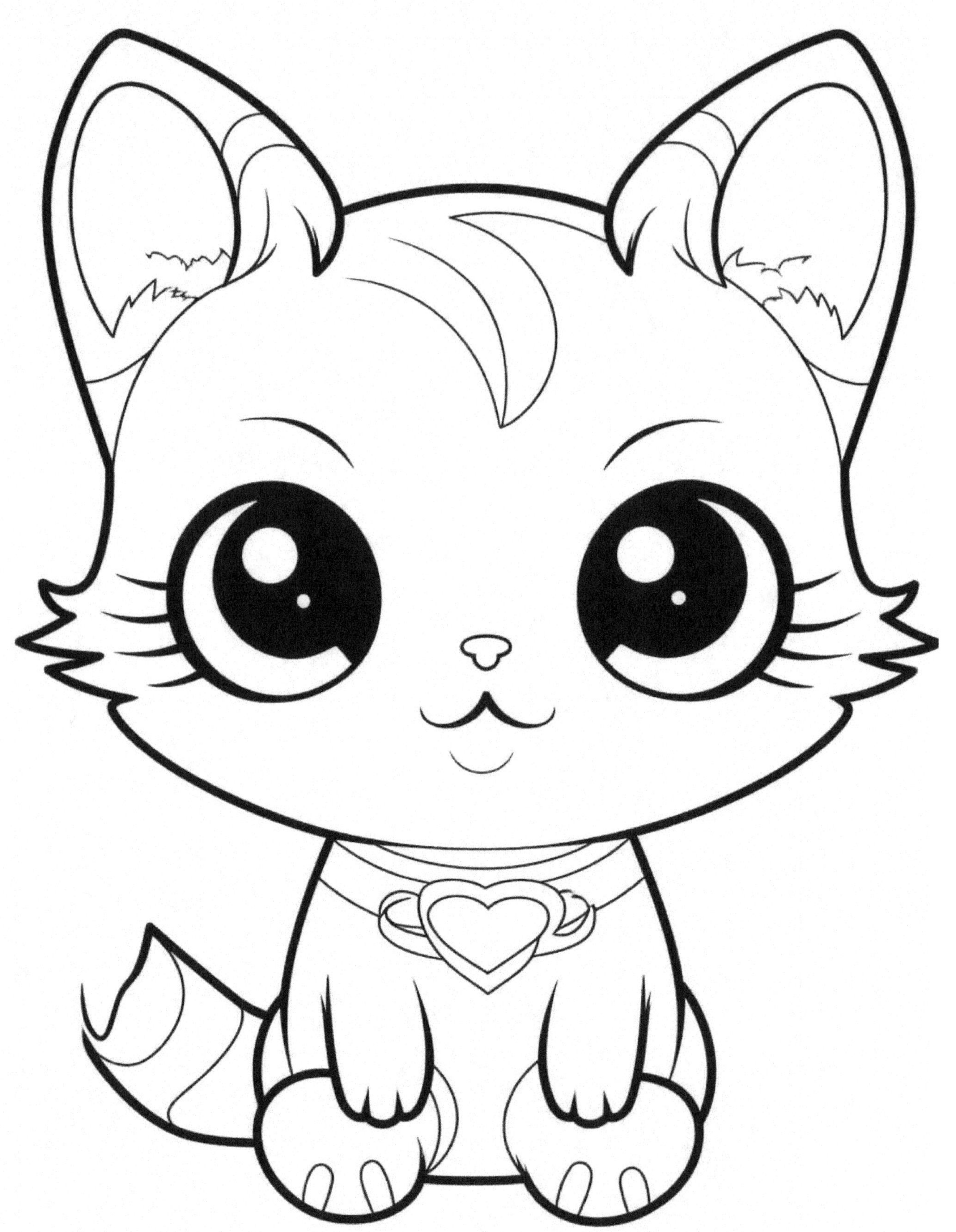

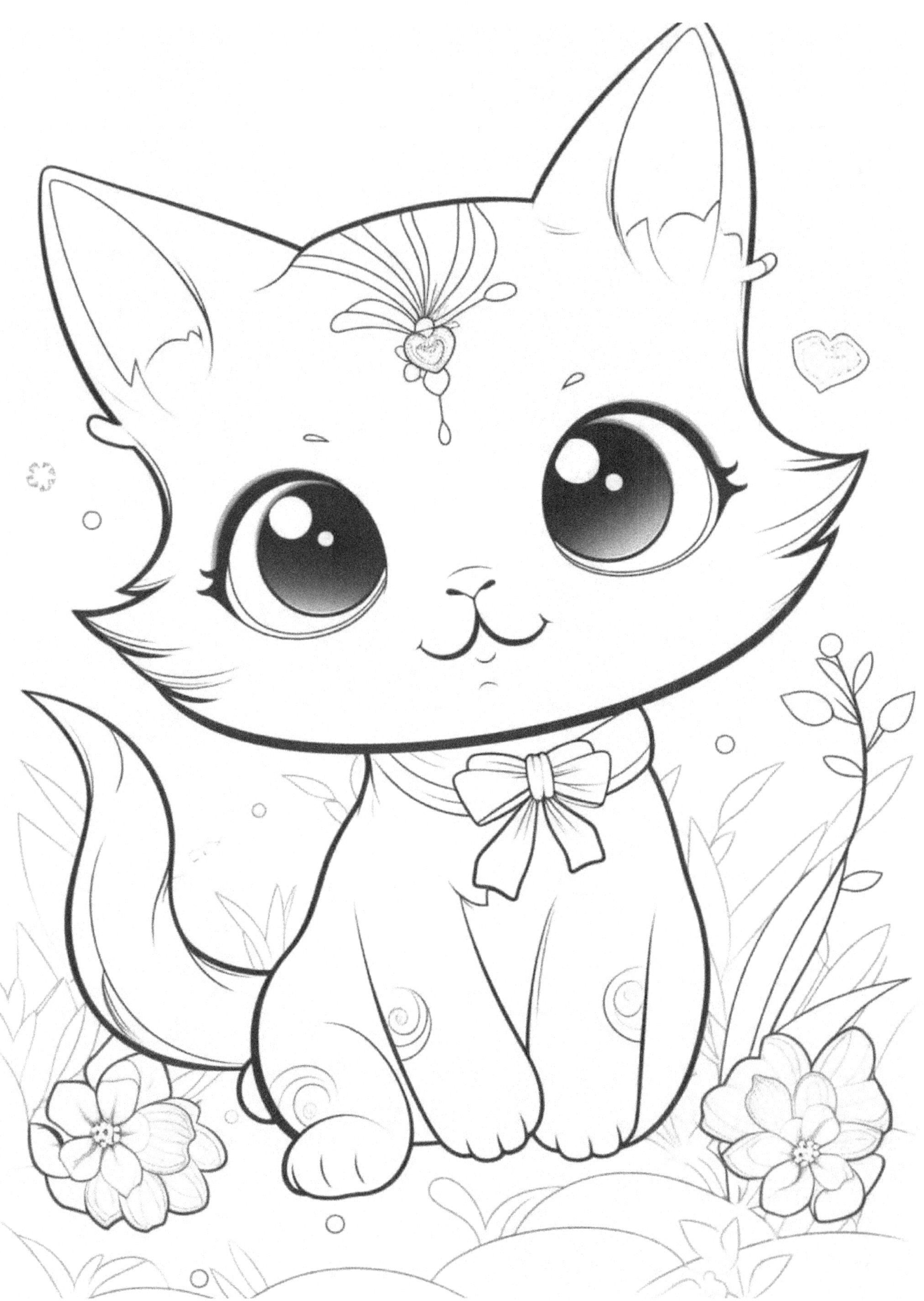

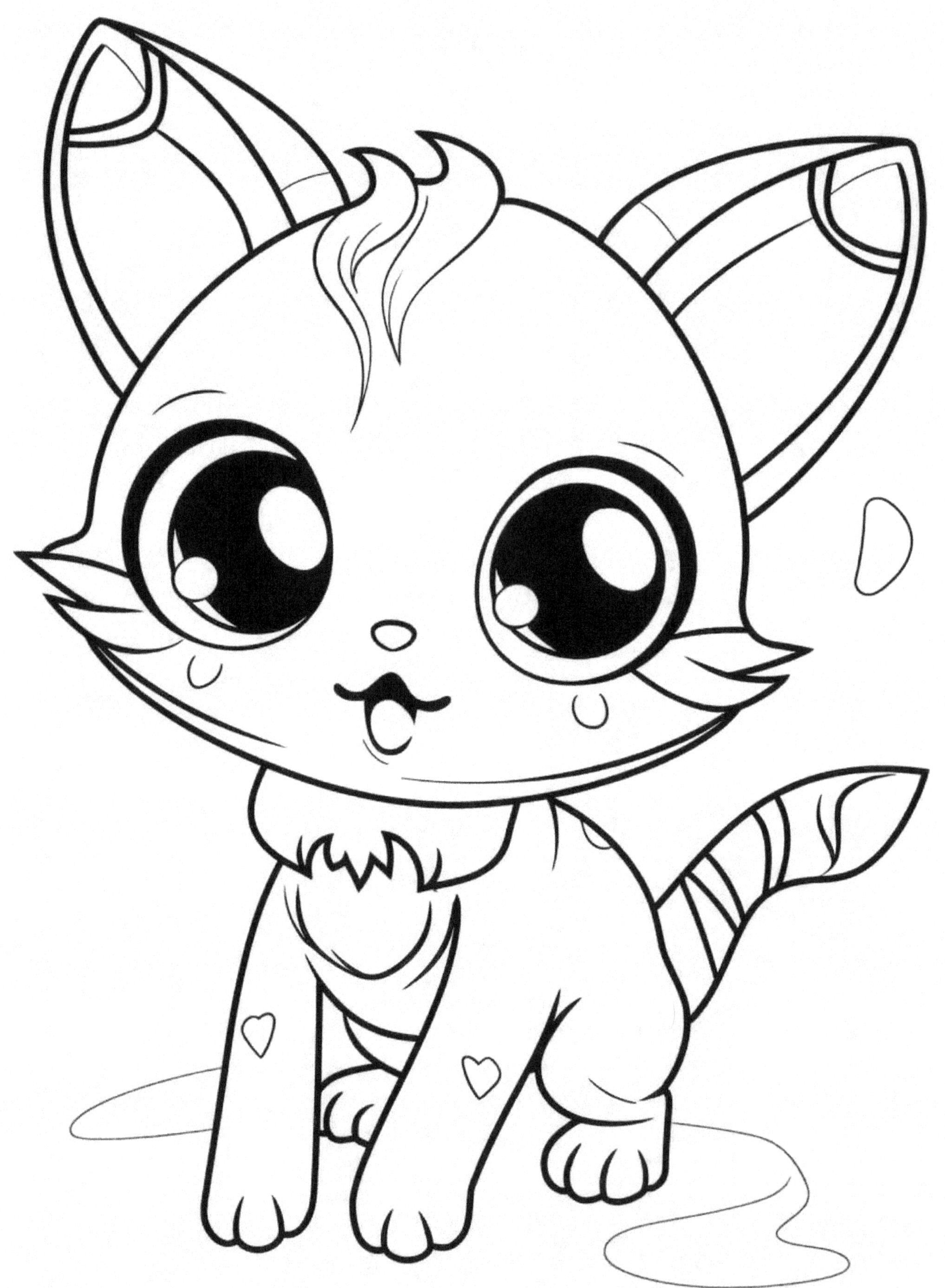

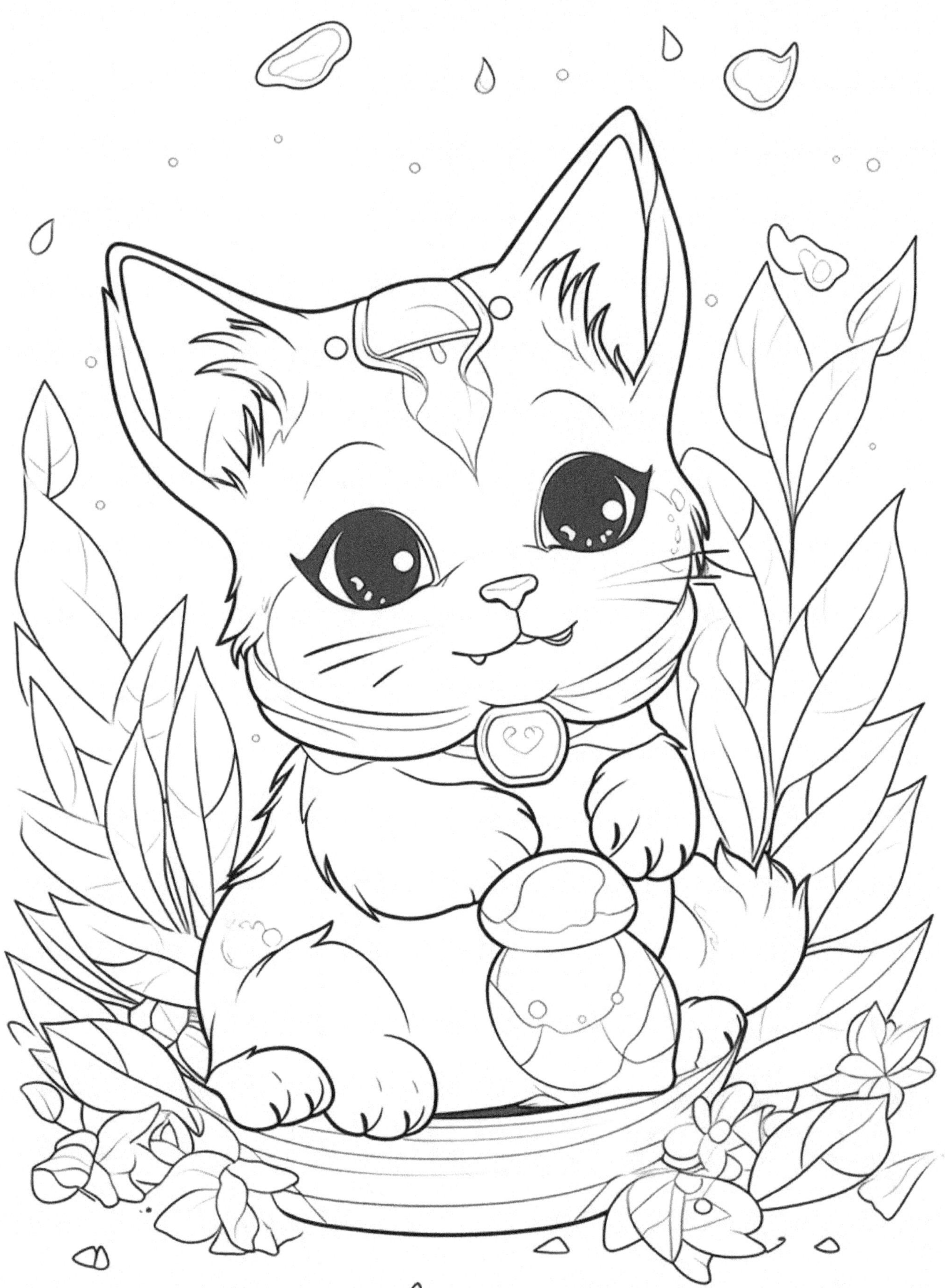

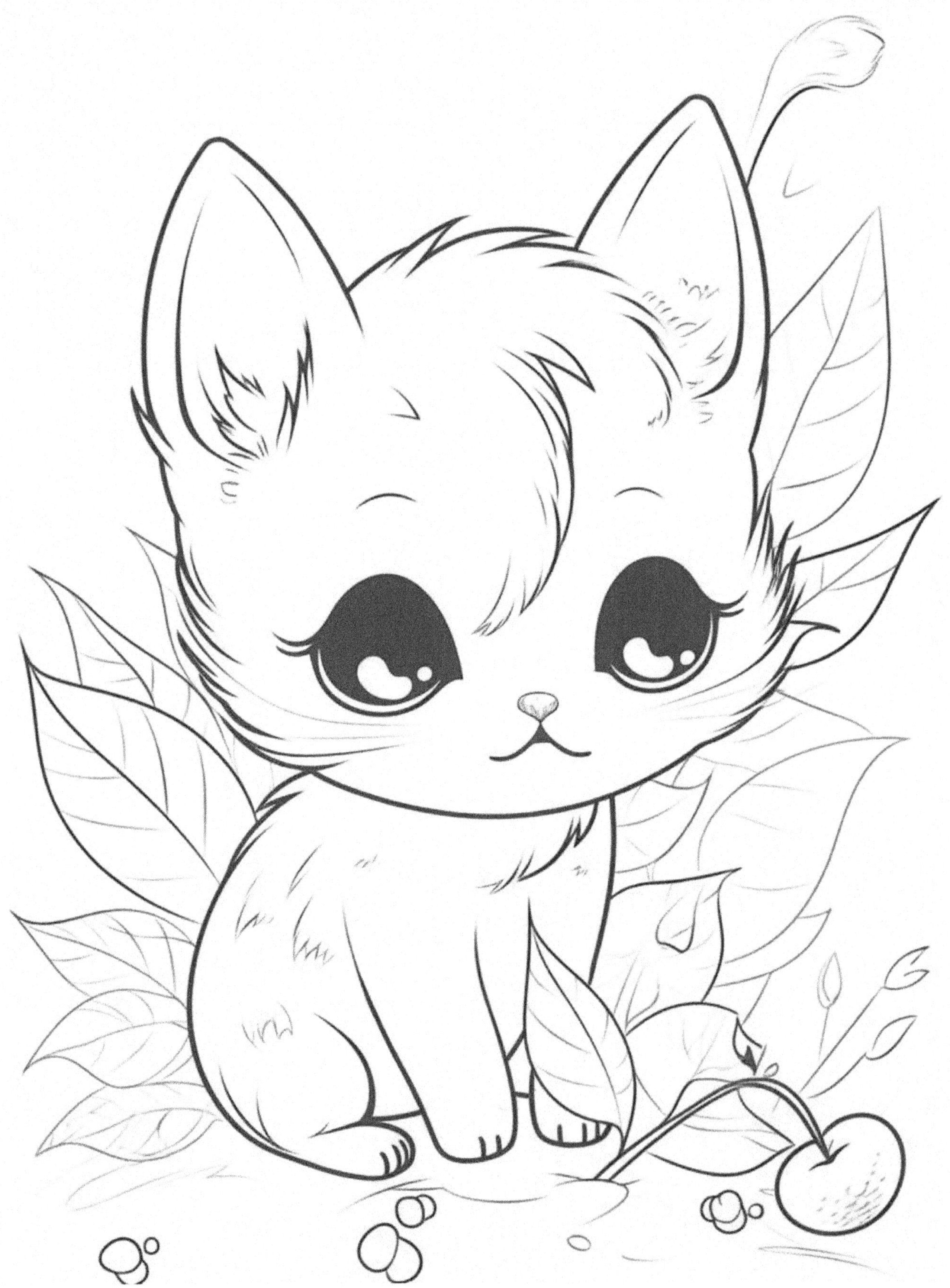

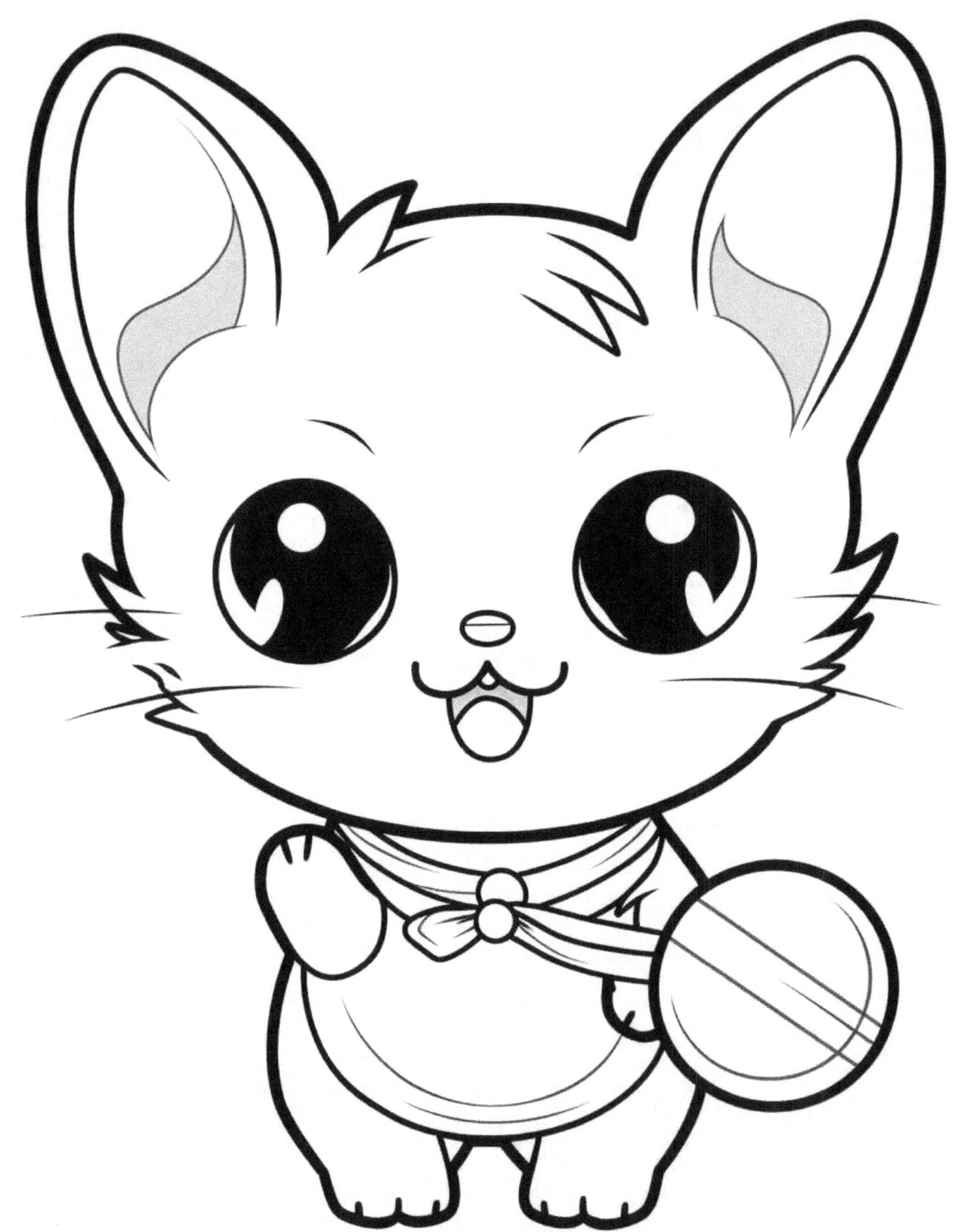

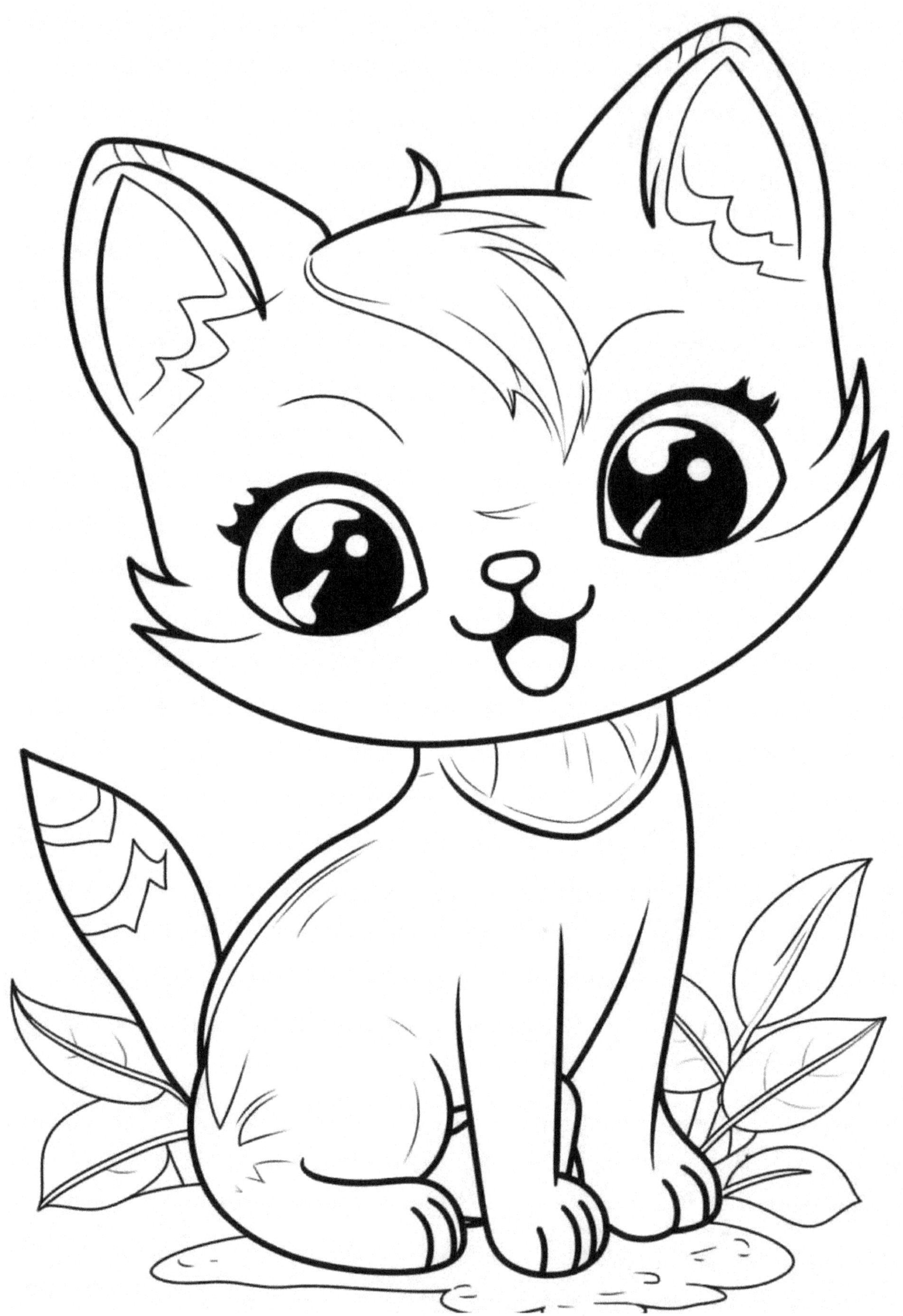

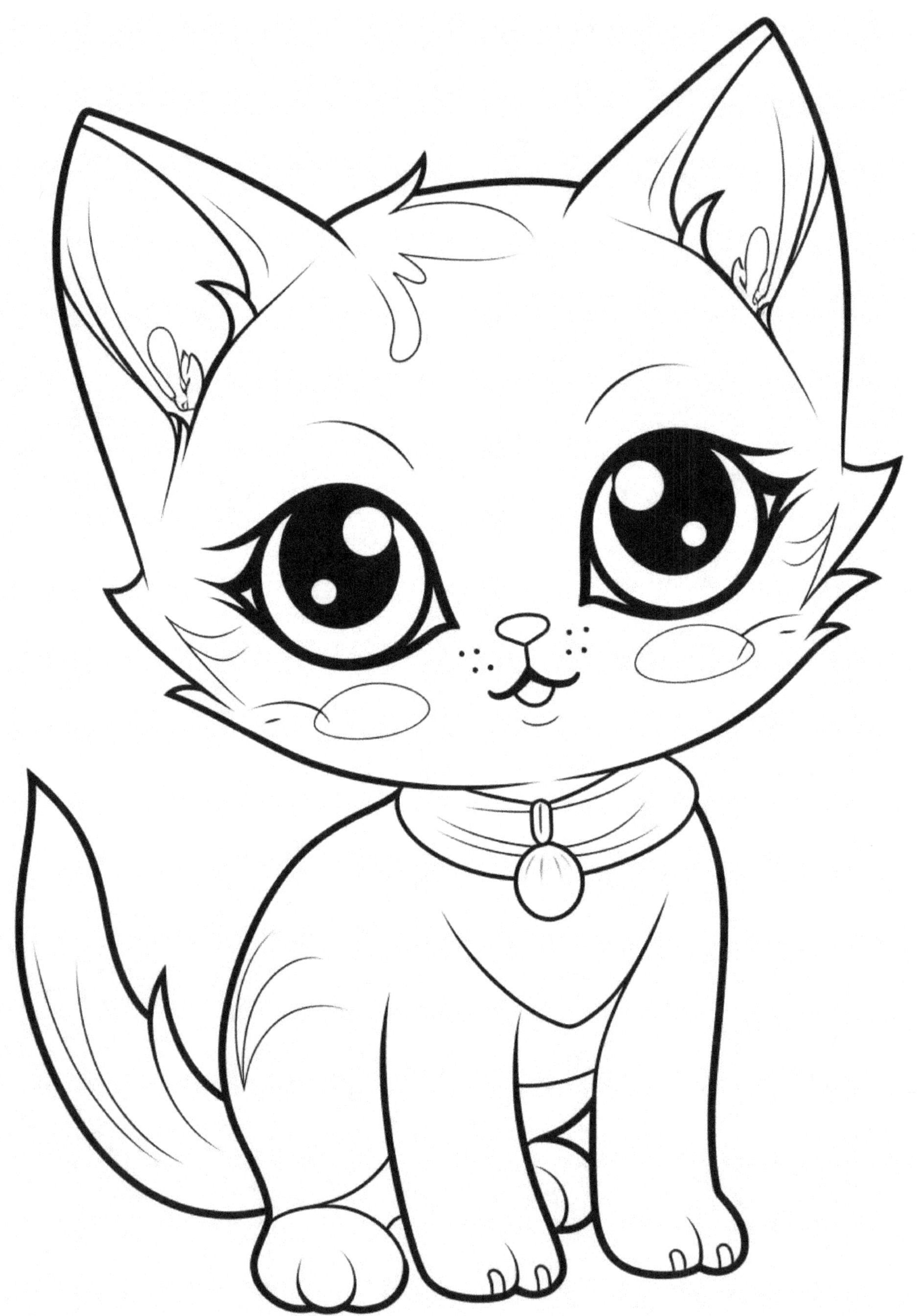

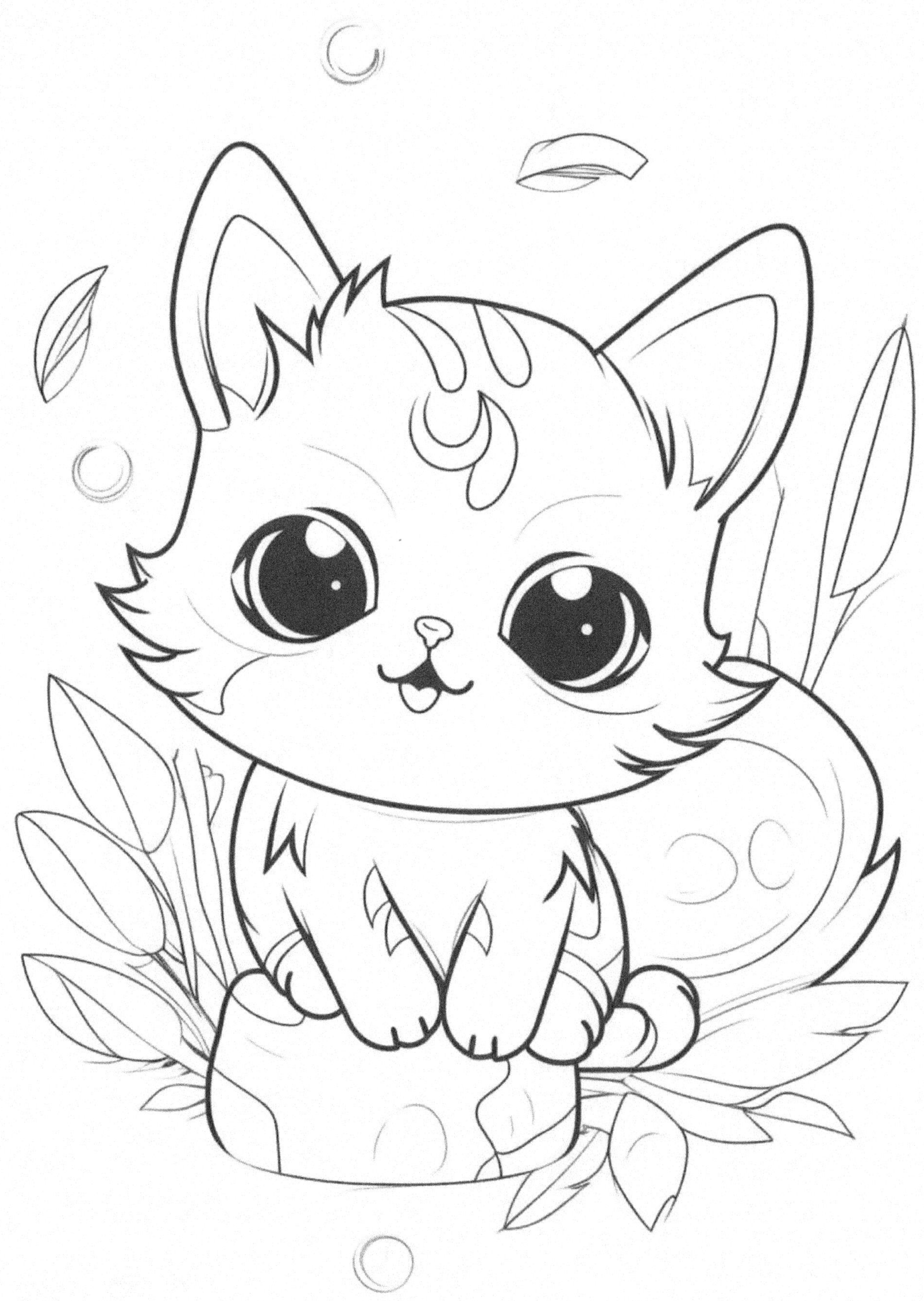

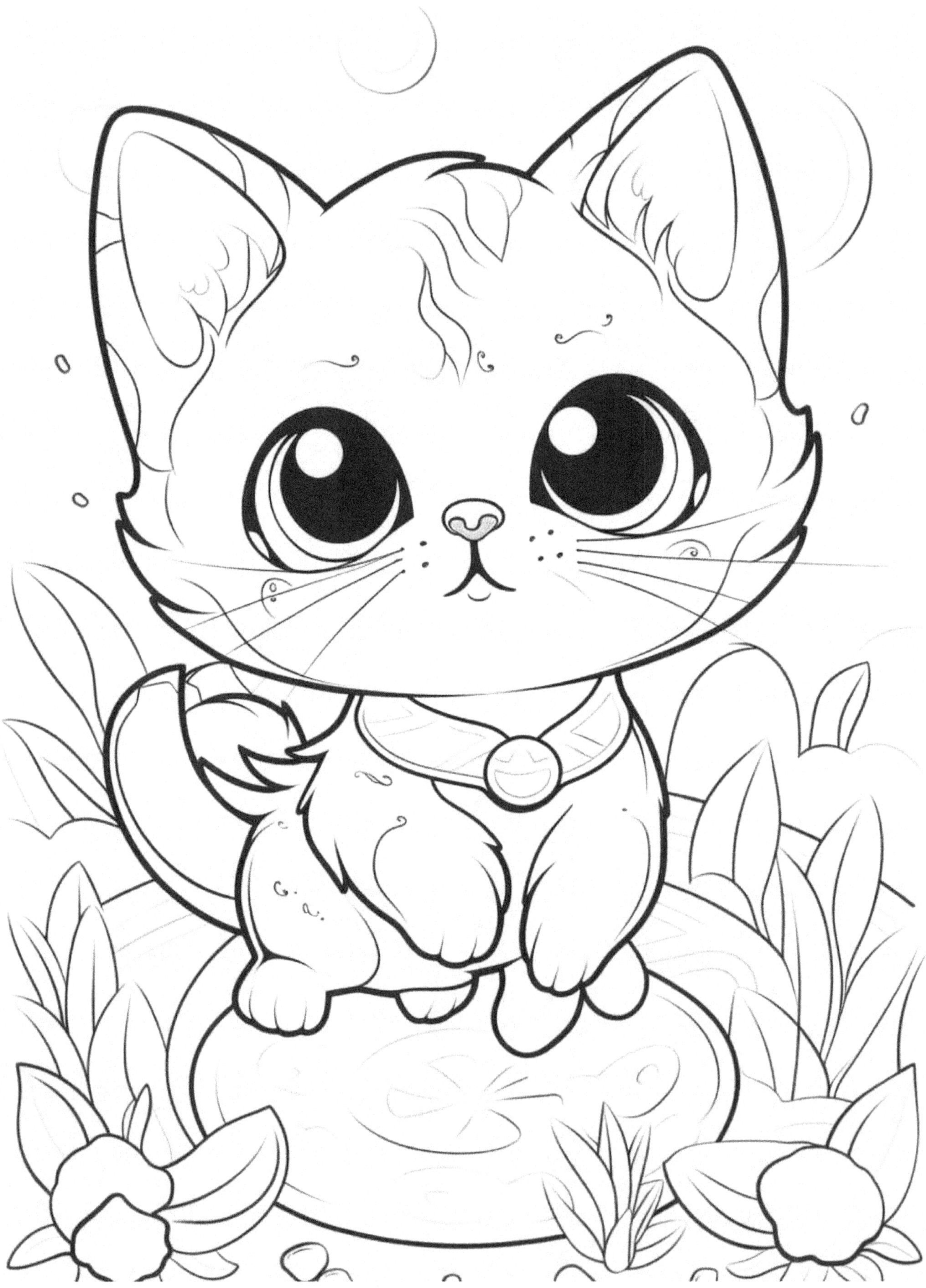

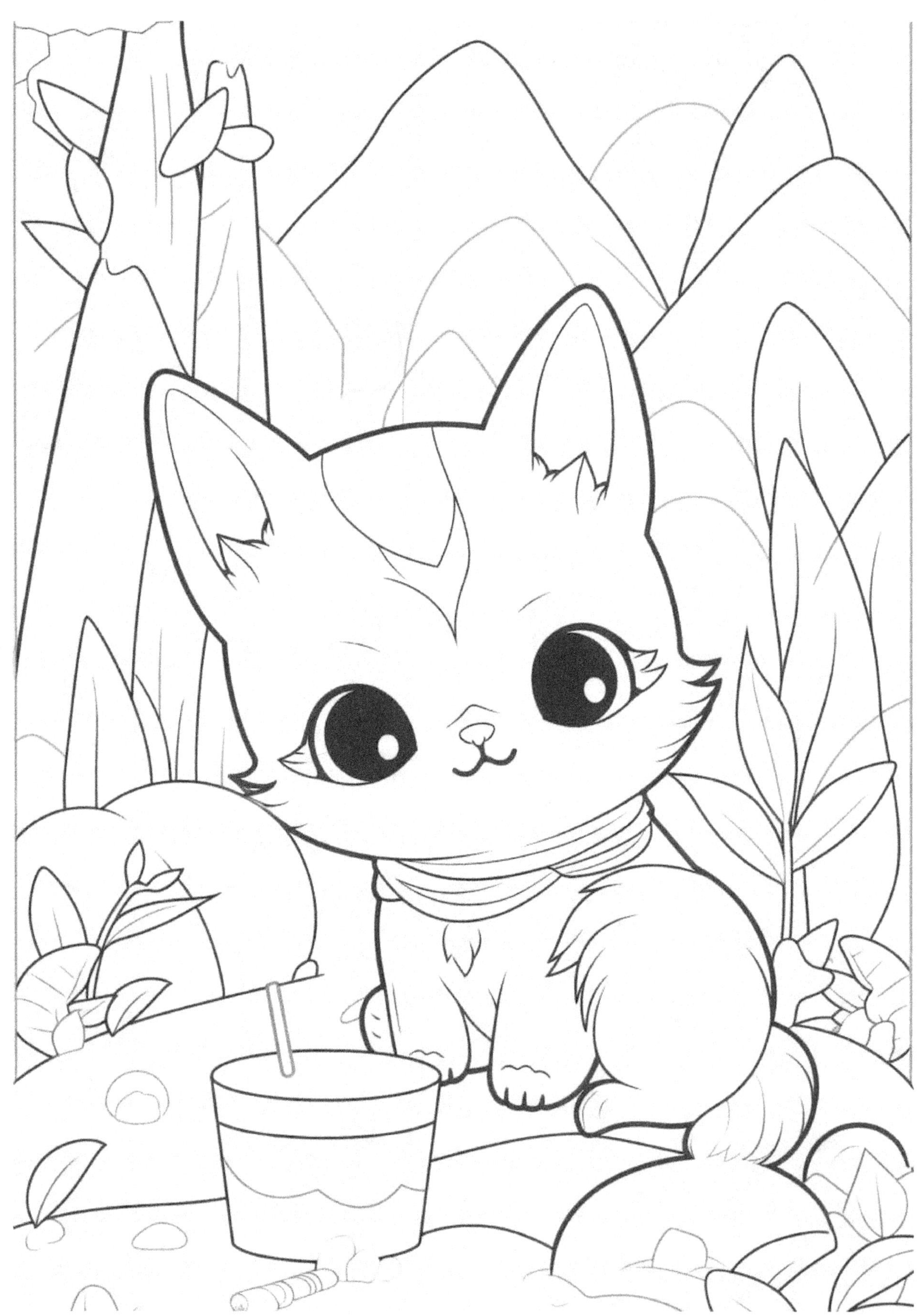

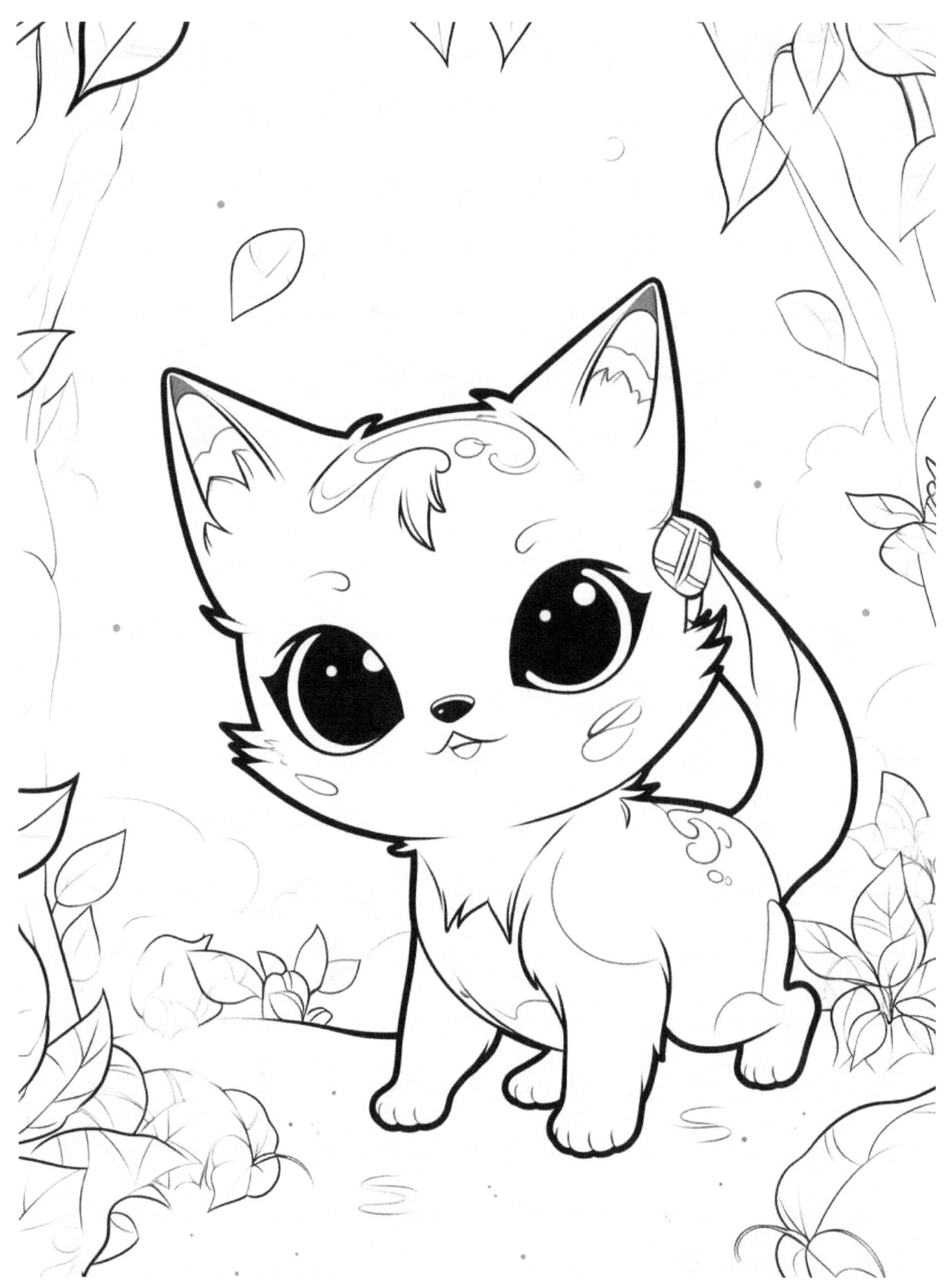

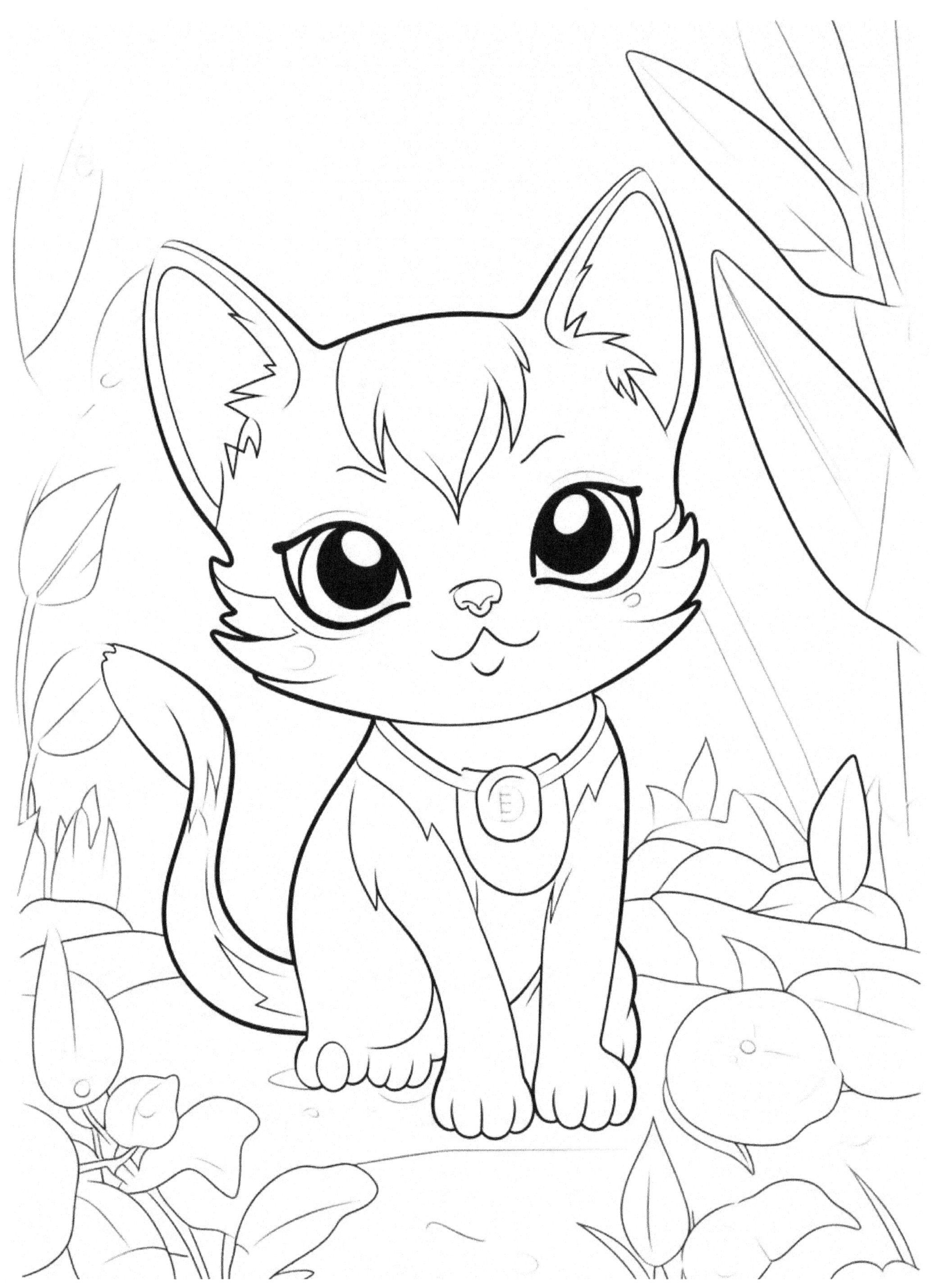

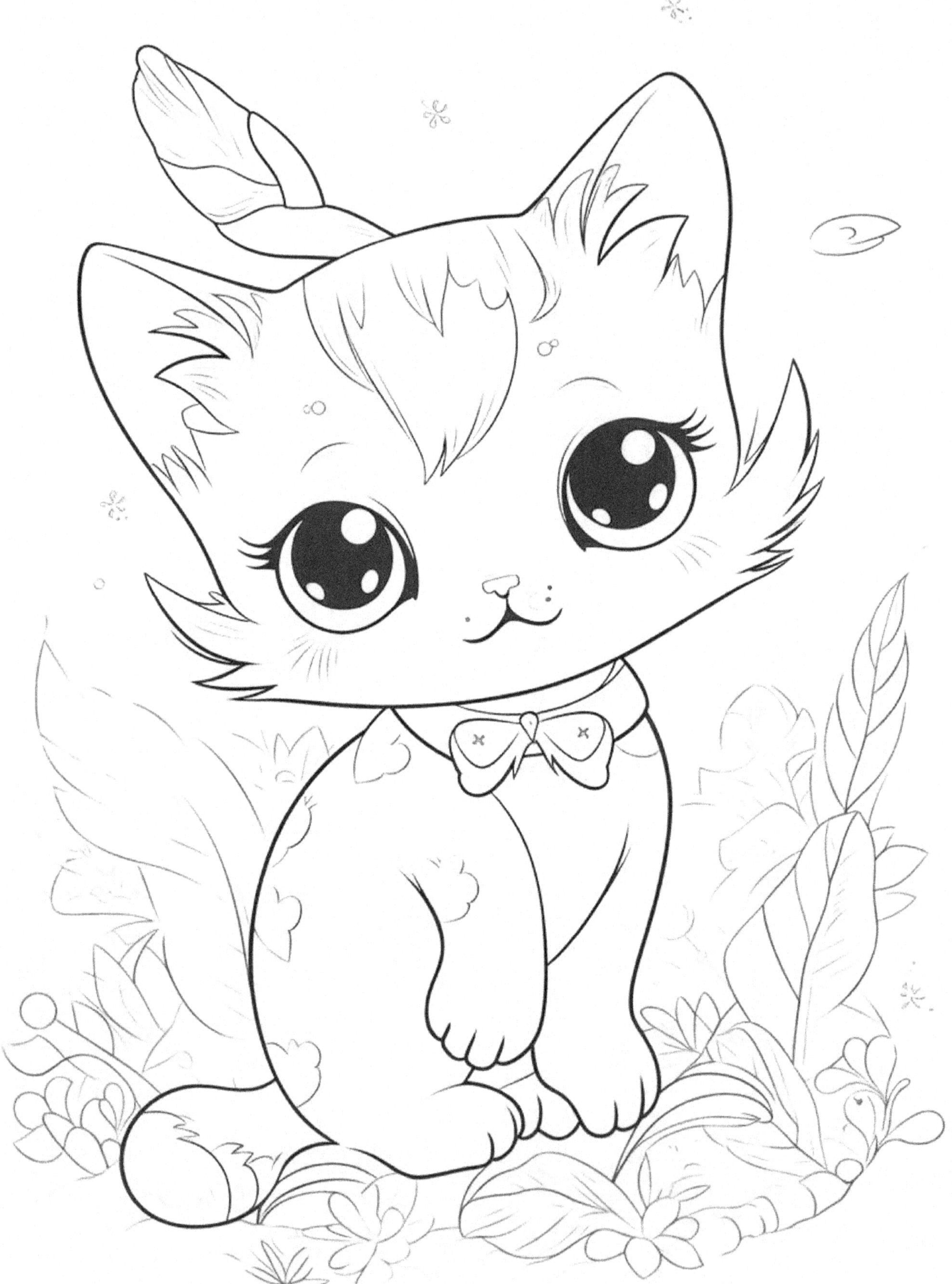